★★★

VOLUME

11

THE
AMERICAN HERITAGE
BOOK OF THE
PRESIDENTS
AND FAMOUS AMERICANS

★ ★ ★ ★ ★

HARRY S. TRUMAN
DWIGHT DAVID EISENHOWER

CREATED AND DESIGNED BY THE EDITORS OF
AMERICAN HERITAGE
The Magazine of History

12-VOLUME EDITION PUBLISHED BY
DELL PUBLISHING CO., INC., NEW YORK, N.Y.

NATIONAL PORTRAIT GALLERY

Harry S. Truman

UNITED PRESS INTERNATIONAL

Dwight David Eisenhower

CONTENTS
OF VOLUME ELEVEN

HARRY S. TRUMAN 905

A PICTURE PORTFOLIO 919

FACTS IN SUMMARY 946

DWIGHT DAVID EISENHOWER 949

A PICTURE PORTFOLIO 961

FACTS IN SUMMARY 988

FAMOUS AMERICANS

Dean Acheson.	933	Ernest Orlando Lawrence	927
Alben W. Barkley	915	John L. Lewis	942
Bernard M. Baruch	933	Douglas MacArthur	943
Omar N. Bradley	984	George C. Marshall	939
James B. Conant	927	Sam Rayburn	932
John Foster Dulles	985	Carl Sandburg	974
Albert Einstein	926	Adlai E. Stevenson	978
William Faulkner	974	Robert A. Taft	971
Enrico Fermi	926	J. Strom Thurmond	943
Robert Frost	975	Arthur H. Vandenberg	932
Ernest Hemingway	975	Henry Wallace	942
J. Edgar Hoover	984	Earl Warren	985

THE THIRTY-THIRD PRESIDENT (1945–1953)

HARRY S. TRUMAN

The 1951 baseball season got under way with all attendant ritual. It began, as usual, in the nation's Capital, in archaic Griffith Stadium, which was decked out for the occasion in the customary festive bunting. The traditionally large Opening Day crowd was on hand; so was the President to throw out the first ball.

On that same April Friday, in New York, another ritual was being performed: the ticker-tape parade. Seven and a half million people turned out under a seven-hundred-ton downpour of colorful debris and cheered themselves hoarse for four hours. The hero for whom this demonstration, the most spectacular in the city's history, was staged was General Douglas MacArthur, who had been relieved of his command in Korea by the President.

As MacArthur's motorcade inched its way along Broadway, President Harry S. Truman stood up in Washington to throw the baseball. There was a second's hush; then some paper cups flew in his direction and a chorus of boos rose from the crowd. Like the echo of thunder in a deep canyon the booing rolled around the old wooden stands; it continued as the President threw the ball; it followed him as he turned, lowered his head, and climbed the steps toward the exit ramp. Not until he had left the ball park did the commotion die down and the baseball game begin.

When the "average-man" President ordered the bigger-than-life hero to leave Korea and come home, he knew what he was letting himself in for; the nationwide veneration expressed for MacArthur and the vilification heaped on Truman came as no surprise. But when it was later suggested that the dismissal had been the most courageous act of his Presidency, Truman disagreed. "Courage didn't have anything to do with it," he said. "General MacArthur was insubordinate and I fired him. That's all there was to it."

Harry S. Truman, photographed by Fritz Henle

"That's all there was to it" was one of Harry Truman's pet phrases. It made the decisions of his administration sound like simple choices between black and white. But the facts indicate otherwise. His Presidency began with the explosion of the atomic bomb and ended with a war in Korea. He was a war President, a postwar President, and a cold-war President. The future of mankind—indeed, whether there would be a future at all—often depended on the course he chose to take. And few of the issues he faced were black or white; most were a cold and subtle gray.

Just as the decisions he made were more complex than he admitted, Truman the man was much more prismatic than he appeared. When Franklin Roosevelt's death made him President, Truman seemed to be an ordinary man suddenly catapulted into a position of awesome power. "Boys," he said to the White House reporters, "if you ever pray, pray for me now." When they called him Mr. President, he said, "I wish you didn't have to call me that." So strong was the average-man image that even those who admired him said that he "rose" to the occasion, that the office made the man.

Two incidents, however, suggest that Truman was not so average after all. He had been President for less than two full days when he phoned an administrative official to inform him of a presidential appointment. The official wanted to know if the President had made that appointment before he died. "No," Truman snapped. "He made it just now." The new Chief Executive had only ten days to prime himself for his first meeting with Russian diplomats. The ambassador to Moscow, Averell Harriman, was understandably distressed: America's growing disagreements with the Soviet Union were subtle and complex, even for the well informed. Two days before the meeting, Harriman called on the President in an effort to prepare him. "I had talked with Mr. Truman for only a few minutes," Harriman recalled, "when I began to realize that the man had a real grasp of the situation. What a surprise and a relief this was! . . . He

knew the facts and sequence of events, and he had a keen understanding of what they meant." So, while the mourning American people saw a bewildered man as their new President, Truman was actually taking over with firmness and perspicacity.

Born on May 8, 1884, in Lamar, Missouri, Truman was afflicted from boyhood with poor eyesight. Bright and sociable, he had many friends, but tired of being a spectator at their games; he could not play because he was afraid of breaking the thick-lensed eyeglasses he had to wear after 1892. By the time he was thirteen or fourteen, he had read every book in the public library at Independence, Missouri, where his family had moved. His favorite subject was history, which he continued to read for the rest of his life. Again and again his debt to history was mentioned in his writings and reflected in his presidential decisions.

His father's financial difficulties around the turn of the century made it impossible for Truman to enter college, and his poor eyesight prevented his admittance to West Point. Until the outbreak of World War I, he worked first at a series of clerical jobs—most of them in Kansas City—and then returned to his parents' farm outside Independence. In August, 1917, the National Guard unit to which he belonged was mobilized, and he served in France as an artillery officer. He was discharged as a captain in May, 1919.

Seven weeks later he married Elizabeth Wallace. He and Bess had been sweethearts since they had been in the same fifth-grade class. Because Truman had had no definite future, he had been reluctant to marry, although they had had an "understanding." When he returned home from the war, he was thirty-five years old and Bess was a year younger. Future or no future, they married. They had one child, Margaret.

Truman and an Army friend, Eddie Jacobson, raised some money and opened a haberdashery in Kansas City. At first they did very well, but their customers—mostly farmers and laborers—were hard hit by the recession of 1921. The shop had to be closed

Harry Truman wore strong eyeglasses from the age of eight. In baseball games, he recalled, "I umpired because I couldn't see well enough to bat."

in 1922, but Truman continued to pay his debts and avoided bankruptcy.

At about the time that the haberdashery was failing, Mike Pendergast, an Army buddy of Truman's and the brother of Kansas City political boss Tom Pendergast, talked Truman into running for district judge (in Missouri an administrative, not a judicial, position). He won and served capably for two years, but suffered his only political defeat in 1924, when he lost his bid for re-election. In 1926, however, "Big Tom" himself guided Truman to victory in a race for chief judge of Jackson County.

Tom was not anxious to have the incorruptible Truman in the United States Senate, but when several faithful Pendergast men refused to run, the boss turned to the judge. Truman won his Senate seat in 1934, and even the anti-Pendergast Kansas City *Star* had to admit that with Truman, "a man of unimpeachable character and integrity," in the Senate, "Missouri [could] expect that its interests [would] be safeguarded and advanced from a national standpoint."

Pendergast was anti-Roosevelt, but Truman voted consistently for New Deal measures. Nevertheless, Truman was regarded in Washington as "the Senator from Pendergast." He found it difficult to establish a rapport with the administration, especially after Pendergast was jailed for income tax evasion in 1939. Frustrated and finding it difficult to make ends meet in Washington, Truman considered not standing for re-election in 1940. But then Missouri Governor Lloyd Stark, once a Pendergast man, publicly repudiated the boss and decided to run for Truman's Senate seat. President Roosevelt preferred Stark and offered Truman an appointment to the Interstate Commerce Commission. Truman's proud mind was made up for him: he *had* to make the race.

But the Pendergast machine was now impotent and could offer him little help. Truman had no money for rallies or radio broadcasts, so he drove around the state in his own car and met the people where they lived or worked. A few Senate colleagues came into Missouri to campaign for Truman. Labor began to support the candidate, and contributions started to trickle in. He narrowly defeated Stark in the primary and won a comfortable plurality in the election.

During the campaign Truman had been struck by the waste and inefficiency he had seen at some of the munitions plants and Army bases he had visited; afterward, he quietly drove through twelve Southern states to see how widespread the problem was. In the next session of Congress he spoke at length about the shoddiness and wastefulness of the defense program. The Senate yawningly established the Special Committee to Investigate the National Defense Program with Truman as chairman. Its purpose was to make certain that the taxpayer was getting matériel that was worth the price he was paying. After Pearl Harbor, the Truman committee became much more important. Without seeking headlines, it made them by exposing corporations that were growing rich on the war by making bad equipment in overstaffed plants. It was estimated that by 1944 the committee had saved the taxpayers approximately fifteen billion dollars. The administration, of course, was no longer dissociating itself from Truman: he had become one of the most respected men in the Senate.

As the Democratic National Convention of 1944 approached, President Roosevelt's candidacy for a fourth term was a foregone conclusion. But there was a powerful drive among many party leaders to drop Vice President Wallace from the ticket. His evangelistic liberalism and his affection for Russia had made many enemies. Plenty of volunteers for the Vice Presidency were available, but none were acceptable to National Chairman Robert Hannegan. He preferred either William O. Douglas, the Supreme Court justice, or Senator Harry S. Truman. Neither wanted the nomination.

On the eve of the vice presidential balloting, Hannegan summoned Truman to his

As this exaggerated cartoon implies, F. D. R.'s mind was not on a running mate in 1944. Busy with the war, he let Democratic National Chairman Bob Hannegan survey the field, and Truman was selected.

suite. The chairman picked up the phone and held it away from his ear. "Bob," boomed the big, unmistakable voice of Franklin Roosevelt, which was clearly audible to Truman, "have you got that fellow lined up yet?" "No," said Hannegan. "He is the contrariest Missouri mule I've ever dealt with." "Well, you tell him," said the President, "that if he wants to break up the Democratic party in the middle of a war, that's his responsibility." Without waiting for a reply, Roosevelt hung up.

"Why the hell didn't he tell me in the first place?" Truman said. Despite the spirited supporters of Henry Wallace, Truman was nominated on the second ballot.

Roosevelt won his fourth term, and Truman moved from his desk in the Senate to the podium. Just after he adjourned that body on April 12, 1945, he was called to the White House. When he arrived he was escorted to Eleanor Roosevelt's study. The First Lady approached him and put her arm around him. "Harry," she said, "the President is dead." It took him a moment to find his voice; then he asked if there was anything he could do for her. "Is there anything *we* can do for *you*?" she responded. "For you are the one in trouble now."

He was indeed. Within months the atomic bomb would blast in the atomic age, the war would end, and the cold war would begin; labor would revolt, Congress would revolt, some Cabinet members would revolt, and Truman would write, "Charlie Ross said I'd shown I'd rather be right than President, and I told him I'd rather be anything than President."

As the defeat of Germany became imminent, the Allied powers found it increasingly difficult to get along with one another. At Yalta, several months before his death, Roosevelt had met with Stalin and Churchill to determine the postwar alignment of Europe. The liberated nations were to be reconstructed as soon as possible, and free elections were to be held to determine the nature of their governments. The United States and Great Britain had fulfilled this agreement in the Low Countries; but in Po-

President Harry Truman looks delighted as U.S. Ambassador Edward R. Stettinius signs the United Nations Charter in 1945. Standing behind Stettinius is Republican Harold E. Stassen, who had helped draft the charter.

land, liberated by the Red army, the democratic leaders in exile were not permitted to return, and a Soviet puppet government was established.

In San Francisco the anti-Fascist nations of the world were converging to write the charter of the United Nations. Russia wanted Poland to be seated. The Western Allies refused, however, because democratic elections had not been held there. The chiefs of staff and a number of Roosevelt's advisers told Truman that if Poland were not seated, Russia would walk out of the San Francisco Conference and the United Nations would be doomed. Ambassador Harriman, however, recommended otherwise. On April 23 he brought Soviet Foreign Minister Vyacheslav Molotov and Ambassador Andrei Gromyko to the White House to meet the new President, who proceeded to issue a tongue-lashing regarding the observance of agreements. "I have never been talked to in my life like this," Molotov said. Truman replied, "Carry out your agreements and you won't get talked to like this."

The Russians gave in a little; so did the United States. A few exiled Poles were taken into the Polish government, and Poland was seated. The United Nations Charter was signed on June 26. Secretary of State Edward R. Stettinius was appointed ambassador to the United Nations, and James

Byrnes, who had hoped for the 1944 vice presidential nomination that Truman had received, was appointed Secretary of State.

Meanwhile, on May 7, the war in Europe ended; and in July President Truman traveled to Potsdam, Germany, to meet with Churchill and Stalin. The principal achievements of this conference were the establishment of territorial lines in Europe and the renewal of the Yalta agreement that the Soviet Union would enter the war against Japan. On such matters as the reconstruction of Poland, the rights of the Western powers to their prewar property in Rumania and Bulgaria, and the presence of American troops in the Mediterranean and the Near East, there was no decision. From such issues sprang the cold war.

At Potsdam President Truman was informed that the first test of an actual atomic bomb had been successful; it was up to him to formalize the unofficial decision to employ it. Truman had learned about the atomic bomb for the first time after becoming President, and he had promptly established a committee of distinguished citizens to study the military and moral issues that the emergence of atomic power would raise. The committee agreed that the bomb should be used against Japan, but could not agree on whether or not the United States atomic secrets should be shared with other nations.

As justifiably complicated as the moral issue of using the bomb has become through the years, at the time whether to use it was the less difficult of the two questions. Available information indicated that although the Allies were closing in on the Japanese islands, the invasion itself would probably take as much as a year at a possible cost of a million Allied casualties. Moreover, the drive toward Japan had been slowed by Japanese suicide pilots. The kamikazes could not have turned the tide of the war, but the tactic was terrifying. Under these circumstances the decision to use the bomb was made. Hiroshima was all but obliterated on August 6; Nagasaki, three days later. The Japanese agreed to surrender on August 14.

But with his advisory committee unable to advise, the question of multilateral or unilateral control of atomic energy was left in Truman's hands. In November, in a message to the United Nations, Truman said, "We are prepared to share, on a reciprocal basis, with other members of the United Nations

detailed information concerning the practical industrial application of atomic energy." But to the surprise of everyone, the Soviet Union voted *Nyet*. "It was," said Truman, "an astonishing thing. All the representatives of the other countries in the world sat in stunned silence. . . . They all expected that the Russians would agree, and so did I. And it left the situation in such a way that everybody lost." The fact was, though nobody knew it then, that the Russians were already learning about atomic energy.

As the shooting war abroad ended, Truman's war with Congress at home began. The nation's wartime economy had to be adapted to peace. To make the conversion and retain stability the President issued, on August 18, a "hold-the-line order," which extended wartime controls on production, wages, and prices. Truman knew his history: wars were invariably followed by inflation, then by bust. The only way to avoid another recession was to calculate the conversion and make it a gradual one.

On September 6 he sent his recommendations to Congress and included suggestions for federal aid to education, an increase in the minimum wage, a medical insurance plan, and civil rights legislation. The uproar in Congress was immediate. "This is the kickoff," said Republican Charles Halleck. "This begins the campaign of 1946."

The principal problem, as Truman saw it, was price control. Although there was plenty of money around, consumer goods were scarce; people willingly paid outrageous prices for a pair of nylon stockings or a coffee pot. To make matters worse, business was hoarding the goods it was producing, waiting for the end of controls. If controls were suddenly dropped, prices would rise even higher; so would the cost of living; so would wage demands. That was the normal inflationary pattern that Truman wanted to avoid. The "compromise" control bill that Congress grudgingly passed was so full of

"Are You Sure You Didn't Miss Anything?" Truman asks after his rocky first year in the Presidency.

loopholes that it was unenforceable. Truman vetoed it, but a stronger bill was not enacted, and the Office of Price Administration went out of business in June, 1946. Predictably, prices soared. By August there were consumer strikes and a public uproar so great that Congress hastily produced a new law calling for a gradual phasing-out of price regulation. It was—and Congress knew it—too late. The administrative machinery of the OPA had been disassembled.

A higher cost of living requires higher wages. No longer hampered by the no-strike laws of wartime and anxious to test the strong right-to-strike legislation passed in the 1930's, organized labor emerged from the war with muscles flexing. By the end of 1945 nine hundred thousand workers were on strike from several industries, and early in 1946 another million joined them.

The most serious threats came from the United Mine Workers and the various railroad unions. John L. Lewis had closed the soft-coal mines in March, 1946, and with factories inoperative and the lights of cities dimming because of fuel shortages, the people would not put up with a shutdown of transportation, too. In April Truman discovered that eighteen of the railmen's twenty major leaders were willing to settle for the contract the government had helped negotiate. The two dissenters were the President's old friends Alvanley Johnston (Brotherhood of Locomotive Engineers) and A. F. Whitney (Brotherhood of Railroad Trainmen). He called them to the White House in early May and erupted: "If you think I'm going to sit here and let you tie up this whole country, you're crazy as hell."

On May 21 Truman seized the coal mines and sent Secretary of the Interior Julius A. Krug to settle with Lewis. The settlement infuriated the mine operators, but they had no choice in the matter, and the miners went back to work.

The railroad strike, meanwhile, was scheduled to begin on May 25. The day before, the President told his Cabinet that he intended to draft the striking employees into the Army and thus compel them to run

Labor leader John L. Lewis, above in an Esquire *cartoon, was a perpetual thorn in Truman's side.*

the trains. On the afternoon of the twenty-fifth, Truman addressed a special session of Congress to ask for the induction bill. Just as he came to that part of the speech, a note was handed to him: "Agreement signed, strike over." Truman asked for the anti-strike legislation anyway, but the Senate defeated the measure.

In October, John L. Lewis acted up again. Engaged in a power struggle with other union leaders, Lewis decided to demonstrate his strength in a battle with the government. Using a minor point in the contract as an excuse, he demanded that negotiations be reopened. When Secretary Krug refused, Lewis said the mine workers would consider the contract void as of November 20. Bristling with anger, the President asked for an injunction, and on November 18 the court ordered the miners not to strike. They struck anyway, and on December 3 the union was fined three and a half million dollars, and Lewis personally, ten thousand.

Truman said that his wife Bess (left) was "the Boss" but that daughter Margaret "bosses her."

Still the strike went on, and the President announced that he would make a radio appeal to the miners. Lewis must have feared that his men were no longer with him, for he ordered the miners back to work.

The public had so soured on organized labor throughout 1946 that Truman's firmness might have stopped or reversed the fast decline in his popularity; but he neutralized the effect by vetoing the antilabor Case bill of 1946. The Eightieth Congress, which was seated in 1947, was, however, a much more conservative legislature and was able to override Truman's veto of the somewhat milder labor-restricting Taft-Hartley Act.

The elections of 1946, which produced the first Republican-controlled Congress since 1930, were a serious repudiation of Truman's administration. Senator J. William Fulbright, then a freshman Democrat, suggested that Truman ought to resign, for the people were obviously against the President. There were many reasons for his unpopularity: labor did not like his toughness, and business did not like his position on controls; the South had no use for his civil

rights proposals, and the North did not like his "style."

Secretary of State Byrnes, who felt that he and not Truman should be President, thought he could make foreign policy unilaterally. Once, when Truman asked him for a report on the Moscow conferences Byrnes had been attending, the Secretary replied that he intended to make a radio broadcast about the talks; Truman could listen to it. On the other hand, Henry Wallace acted as if he were Secretary of State, when in fact he was Secretary of Commerce. While Byrnes was standing firm in discussions with the Soviet diplomats, Wallace was criticizing that firmness. When Wallace attributed his own "neither pro-British . . . nor pro-Russian" attitude to the President, Truman had to fire him, although he "hated to do it."

Byrnes's resignation—which Truman probably requested—came in April, 1946, but did not become effective until his replacement, General George C. Marshall, returned from China in January, 1947. Marshall's frustrating China mission reflected the worldwide situation after the war. In the Orient as in Europe, the Axis had been defeated by uncomfortable alliances of potential antagonists. After the war had ended, the old lines had been redrawn. General Marshall, anxious to pledge American dollars to a peaceful China, was unable to effect a coalition between Chiang Kai-shek's Nationalists and the Communists. One by one the formerly Nazi occupied nations of Eastern Europe had become little more than Soviet colonies. In Iran, where the Allies had maintained several bases, the Russians refused to evacuate according to agreement. In Greece the opposing forces—one Communist, one royalist—were at each other's throats as soon as the British withdrew.

In August, 1946, Russia made a new move in the Middle East. Soviet troops massed along the Turkish border to "protect" Turkey's Black Sea coast. In a note handed to the Soviet ambassador, the policy that would become the Truman Doctrine was foreshadowed: "It is the firm opinion of this government [the United States] that Turkey should continue to be primarily responsible for the defense of the Straits [the Bosporus and the Dardanelles]. Should the Straits become the object of attack or threat of attack by an aggressor, the resulting situation would constitute a threat to international security . . . ." An American naval task force was sent on "routine training maneuvers" off the Turkish coast. And early in 1947 Truman asked Congress for huge sums for aid to Greece and Turkey. That, essentially, was the Truman Doctrine. Its ideological premise was "containment." It told the Soviet Union that it could expand no farther. It was a strong statement, but it placed the initiative for starting a war squarely in Russian hands.

The Truman Doctrine was not universally applicable. In many places, including Italy, France, the Low Countries, and Scandinavia, the Communists were well organized

TRUMAN LIBRARY

The ancient vase above was a gift from the Greek people in appreciation of the Truman Doctrine.

and operated legally. So long as these nations remained impoverished, the possibility of Communist dominance was great.

On June 5, 1947, Secretary of State Marshall said in a speech at Harvard University that the policy of the United States was not directed against a country or an idea, but "against hunger, poverty, desperation, and chaos. Its purpose should be the revival of a working economy in the world. . . ." The United States would offer all the funds necessary to nations that wanted to reconstruct their economies. By implication, this American economic aid was also to be made available to the countries of Eastern Europe; but Russia denounced the Marshall Plan as an "imperial" plot to enslave Europe.

The British historian Arnold Toynbee has written that the most significant achievement of the modern era was not the discovery of atomic power but the attention lavished on the world's poorer nations by the more privileged ones. The Marshall Plan distributed more than twelve billion American dollars to the people of Europe for reconstruction. There were, certainly, some strings attached, but they did not limit the development of freedom and prosperity.

Truman's efforts to avoid war were challenged in June, 1948, when the Russians closed off the autobahn through the Soviet occupation zone in Germany, blocking Allied access to Berlin. Although it was obviously a hostile move, the blockade was a clever diplomatic ploy, for it placed in American hands the responsibility of making the first military move. Truman quickly turned the dare around: he began sending airplanes—carrying supplies—over the Soviet zone and into West Berlin. This put it to the Soviets to fire the first shot, and they did not.

Despite his successes and imaginativeness in foreign policy, Truman was still not getting along with the Eightieth Congress. It had defeated or ignored most of his Fair Deal proposals; it had, against Truman's wishes, cut the budget and passed tax reductions. And Congress was only one of Truman's troubles as his first term approached its end. As Arthur Krock wrote in *The New*

York Times in April, 1948: "A President whose defeat at the next poll is generally prophesied faces difficulties in performing his office that conceivably bring disaster. . . . At this writing, the President's influence is weaker than any President's has been in modern history."

Truman had decided to seek a four-year term of his own, and the decision prompted a variety of responses. Radicals were appalled, reactionaries shocked, regular Democrats gloomy, and regular Republicans joyful. The left, led by Henry Wallace, organized a third party to fight for the Presidency. The South, dismayed by Truman's strong civil rights proposals, defected and ran South Carolina Governor Strom Thurmond as the Dixiecrat (States' Rights) candidate. The remaining Democrats, having been unable to convince General Dwight D. Eisenhower to become their candidate, had no choice but to accept Truman and look forward to inevitable defeat. The Republicans nominated Thomas Dewey, governor of New York. By selecting a moderate, the G.O.P. did not have to campaign against the New Deal—which meant that it did not have to run against the memory of Franklin Roosevelt. Indeed, the Republican platform called for such New Dealish measures as a national health plan, civil rights legislation, a federal housing bill, and extensions of Social Security coverage.

The President appeared before his battered party to accept its nomination. No one had mentioned the word "win" with any conviction. But Harry Truman said: "Senator [Alben] Barkley and I will win this election and make these Republicans like it—don't you forget that."

Next Truman announced his strategy: "On the 26th day of July, which out in Missouri we call 'Turnip Day,' I am going to call Congress back and ask them to pass laws to halt rising prices, to meet the housing crisis—which they are saying they are for in their platform. . . . Now my friends, if there is any reality behind that Republican platform, we ought to get some action from a short session of the Eightieth Congress.

They can do this job in fifteen days, if they want to do it. They will still have time to go out and run for office." There was no way for Congress to avoid Truman's trap. If the legislators passed his proposals, they would increase the President's strength; if they ignored them, they would remain the "do-nothing Eightieth Congress." They chose to do nothing, and Truman made the Congress itself a principal election issue.

After the July "turnip session," Truman assumed an optimism shared by almost no one. Although he was the incumbent, he was the underdog, and regular Democratic contributors saw no sense in throwing good money after bad. To reach as many people as he could, as cheaply as he could, the President set out on two major, and several short, whistle-stop train trips, stopping wherever enough people had gathered to hear him. While Tom Dewey was eloquently stating idealistic abstractions, Truman folksily ranted and raved—not so much against his opponent, not even so much against the Eightieth Congress, as against the people themselves. "If," he harangued, "you stay at home, as you did in 1946, and keep these reactionaries in power, you will deserve every blow you get. . . ." In Albuquerque, New Mexico, he later recalled, he was making such a speech when "some big voice way up in the corner of that 7,000 people auditorium said, 'Give 'em hell, Harry!' Well, I never gave anybody hell—I just told the truth on these fellows and they thought it was hell!" But the polls still forecast a landslide for Dewey.

Of election night, Truman later said, "At six o'clock I was defeated. At ten o'clock I was defeated. Twelve o'clock I was defeated. Four o'clock I had won the election. And the next morning . . . in St. Louis, I was handed this paper which said, 'DEWEY DEFEATS TRUMAN!' Of course, he wished he had, but he didn't and that's all there was to it!" There was something else to it: Congress was Democratic once again.

Foreign policy continued to occupy most of Truman's attention in his second term. World War III never came, but times were tense. The tension produced a major domestic issue in the United States: "loyalty." The result was one of the most appalling periods in the nation's history.

A democracy has the right—the obligation—to protect itself from those who would subvert it. But the "loyalty" crusade of the late 1940's and early 1950's was undemocratic. Investigators who appointed themselves to protect the Constitution thought the way to do it was to ignore that document.

In the years that followed the war, hundreds of government employees were fired on the basis of often anonymous reports alleging that they were or had been Communists, or had associated with Communists. They were deprived of their right to confront their accusers. They were not even told who their accusers were.

In 1948 the House Un-American Activities Committee, which Truman called the most "un-American activity in the whole government," sought and won the imprisonment of ten Hollywood screen writers for contempt of Congress. The writers were so cited because they had employed their constitutional rights: they had insisted on confronting their accusers; they had declined to testify against themselves; they had pointed out that under the American judicial system there was no such thing as "guilt by association." Whether any of the writers were Communists was not established—it was not illegal to be a Communist anyway. If they were in contempt of Congress, Congress was in contempt of the Constitution.

There had been a threat of internal subversion, and there can be little doubt that the espionage of the British spy Klaus Fuchs and of the Americans Ethel and Julius Rosenberg facilitated the Soviet mastery of atomic energy; but the security of the nation was not aided by the purges. A peak of absurdity was reached in 1950 when Senator Joseph McCarthy of Wisconsin, who had been voted "worst" United States senator by the Washington press corps just a few years before, found himself facing sure defeat in his bid for re-election. Looking for an issue to make his constituents forget his

ALBEN W. BARKLEY

Nominated by acclamation as President Truman's running mate in 1948, Alben Barkley of Kentucky told the cheering delegates, "I did not come here as a candidate; I did not become one after I got here, and I was not one." He left unsaid what many knew: as a liberal member of Congress since 1913 and Democratic leader in the Senate for more than a decade, he had been a vice presidential possibility for twenty years. He had wanted the office, and others had wanted him to have it. Some Democrats had even tried to get him to run against Truman in 1948, but he had resisted all attempts to become any sort of a candidate without the blessing of the President. Truman wanted Justice William Douglas to be the vice presidential nominee. He thought Barkley, at seventy, was too old. But when Justice Douglas refused the President's offer, Truman agreed to Barkley, who thus became the oldest Vice President of the United States, and one of the most popular. His grandson called him the Veep, and the nickname stuck—to the office as well as to Barkley. A widower, he was the only Vice President to marry in office. He and Truman set a high standard of working relations between a Chief Executive and a Vice President, but in 1952, when a new presidential candidate had to be found, Truman still felt that Barkley's age made him ineligible, and other Democrats agreed. Barkley was re-elected to the Senate and died in 1956.

dismal performance in Washington, he seized on the internal-security threat. As a result of his totally groundless accusations, scores of men lost their jobs, were degraded before their families and neighbors, had to change their names and cities of residence. But not one Communist or fellow traveler was found, not one spy convicted, not one person even indicted for a crime.

"Ask almost any school child," McCarthy advised, "who the architect of our Far Eastern policy is, and he will say 'Owen Lattimore.'" Lattimore, a Johns Hopkins professor and frequent missionary for the State Department, was, according to McCarthy, "the top Russian espionage agent" in the State Department. When Senator Millard Tydings of Maryland produced an FBI report showing that Lattimore could not have been a Communist at any time, McCarthy turned his attention to Tydings, who was running for re-election. McCarthy

had a fake photograph made showing the senator engaged in friendly conversation with Communist Earl Browder. Tydings' defense of Lattimore, McCarthy said, was only a diversionary trick to cloud his own Communist activities. That sort of logic infected Maryland no less than the rest of the country; Tydings was defeated.

The hysteria was translated into legislation in the McCarran act of 1950. Essentially, the bill required all Communists to register with the Justice Department (this, according to Truman, was like passing a law to make thieves report to the sheriff); provided for the deportation of any alien who had ever been a Communist; and prohibited employment of Communists or their dupes in positions relating to national defense. "It was," as Cabell Phillips has written, "a dragnet such as any dictator might envy." Truman vetoed the McCarran Internal Security Act, declaring that most

Private citizen Harry Truman returned periodically to his favorite presidential retreat, the Florida Keys. Above, with grandsons, Clifton and William Daniel, he dedicates the Truman Bridge at Duck Key in 1964; at right he relaxes at Key West.

916

of its provisions were unconstitutional. Congress passed it over his veto. (In 1965, the Supreme Court ruled the major part of the McCarran act—the registration provision—unconstitutional.)

McCarthy's power, meanwhile, seemed to be without limits. After the outbreak of the Korean War, the senator declared that General George C. Marshall, who had just resigned as Secretary of State, was the leading Communist in the United States. A resolution condemning McCarthy for the absolutely groundless accusation never got out of the Senate Rules Committee, and the senator who had introduced it, Democrat William Benton of Connecticut, was defeated when he ran for re-election.

Normally the nation unites behind its President in times of international tension. But the Red Scare of the late 1940's had split America in two. When the troops of North Korea invaded democratic South Korea in 1950, half the country blamed the "infiltrated" Truman administration for the circumstances that had allowed the attack to happen. Most of the other part doubted that American involvement in Korea was necessary.

After World War II, the United States and Russia, according to the agreements made at Potsdam, had jointly liberated and occupied Japanese-held Korea. The dividing line was the thirty-eighth parallel. South Korea had had its elections; North Korea had not. China, meanwhile, had been fighting a civil war with the result that in 1949 Chiang Kai-shek was forced to evacuate the mainland and retreat to Formosa. When the North Koreans crossed the border into the South, Truman's containment doctrine was put to the test in the Far East.

Truman sent American planes and ships to Korea on June 24, just hours after the invasion had taken place. That day the Security Council of the United Nations examined the events and declared that the invasion constituted an act of armed aggression. The council was in a position to convert Truman's unilateral decision into a United Nations action because the Soviet Union (which could have vetoed the resolution) was at the time boycotting sessions.

General Douglas MacArthur, then ranking officer in the Far East and military governor of Japan, was placed in command of the Korean operation, and from early in the conflict he disagreed with United Nations strategy, which was containment, not destruction, of the aggressor.

Truman's containment policy had worked well in Europe. The Marshall Plan and its extension, Point Four, were rebuilding the Western democracies. The Berlin Airlift had successfully called Russia's bluff, and the blockade of the autobahn had been removed in May, 1949. That same spring the North Atlantic Treaty Organization had been formed by the United States, Great Britain, France, Canada, Belgium, the Netherlands, Luxembourg, Italy, Denmark, Norway, Iceland, and Portugal. The treaty stated that an attack on one would be considered an attack on all and integrated the European defenses of all members.

But in Korea the problem was more complicated. The Russians were not actively involved; neither were the Chinese. But the chance of their intervention was great, and this possibility controlled United Nations strategy.

MacArthur insisted that the Chinese were not going to intervene and that thus there was no reason to limit Allied military action to the South. But as the United Nations forces neared the Yalu River, which separated North Korea from Manchuria, China did intervene; its troops poured across the border and pushed the Allies south of the thirty-eighth parallel.

United Nations orders maintained that all fighting was to be done in or over Korea; the war was not to be introduced into Chinese Manchuria. This presented MacArthur with the frustration of having planes from Chinese bases assault United Nations depots, supply lines, and troops and then retreat to their sanctuary north of the Yalu. By openly criticizing this state of affairs, MacArthur was not only publicly rebuking the Commander in Chief, the joint chiefs of staff, and the United Nations, he was informing the enemy of what was *not* going to be done. As the general began making public statements that were critical of his superiors and writing to the joint chiefs of staff complaining about official policy, Truman responded that he was sympathetic, but that he was losing patience with MacArthur.

On March 20, 1951, the United Nations drafted a proposal for a negotiated settlement of the war, and a copy was sent to MacArthur. In an extraordinary gesture, the general made in a public statement his own offer to negotiate. His plan completely disregarded the official statement made by the President and the United Nations.

Truman considered firing MacArthur then, but hesitated. A few days later, however, on April 5, House Minority Leader Joe Martin read a letter to the House from MacArthur, in which the commander again attacked the official policy of the United Nations. MacArthur had been ordered by the joint chiefs not to make any policy statements without clearance. Twice within ten days he disobeyed that order. On April 10, Truman ordered him to come home.

MacArthur had challenged the constitutional premise that military power is subject to civilian rule in the United States. Despite the hero's welcome that he received, MacArthur was not exonerated. The calls for impeachment of the President died out when Senate hearings revealed that Truman had been on firm constitutional grounds. MacArthur did not receive the presidential nomination he probably wanted, and Truman withstood the ball park boos and another year in the office he had had enough of.

Long-time Speaker of the House Sam Rayburn once said that as President, his friend Harry Truman had been "right on all the big things, wrong on all the little ones." Frankly corny and at times crude, Truman conducted what was probably the most liberal administration in the nation's history, but he surrounded himself with political hacks who were corrupt and inept, and he stood by them when they were denounced. One day he could be playing "Missouri Waltz" on the piano for foreign dignitaries; the next he could be proposing legislation so visionary that it would not be enacted until the 1960's (the Civil Rights Act of 1964 and Medicare of 1965). When a Washington music critic was harsh in a review of Margaret Truman's singing, the President threatened to punch him in the nose. Yet that same Harry Truman was, according to Arthur Krock of *The New York Times*, the only President from Woodrow Wilson through Lyndon Johnson who never took a journalist's criticism personally and never held a grudge.

In the final year of the Truman administration, Winston Churchill visited the United States. He had an admission for Truman: "The last time you and I sat across a conference table was at Potsdam. I must confess, sir, I held you in very low regard. I loathed your taking the place of Franklin Roosevelt. I misjudged you badly. Since that time, you more than any other man, saved Western civilization."

Truman was snubbed by Eisenhower at the latter's inauguration; forgotten, apparently, was Truman's offer to step down in favor of the general in 1948. He went home to Independence to start a library and to refight all his battles in his memoirs. Senator McCarthy implied that he was a traitor and subpoenaed him to appear at a congressional investigation. Truman refused. The Korean War was settled, the MacArthur furor died down, McCarthy was censured; in foreign policy Eisenhower repudiated little that Truman had done. His reputation began to rise as the "big things" lasted and the "little things" passed into insignificance.

On a 1964 television program based on his Presidency, Truman recalled: "The day I left Washington, I wrote my daughter Margaret a letter. . . . And it said this: 'There is an epitaph in Boot Hill cemetery in Arizona which reads, "Here lies Jack Williams. He done his damnedest! What more can a person do?"' Well, that's all I could do. I did my damnedest, and that's all there was to it!"

—DAVID JACOBS

A PICTURE PORTFOLIO

*On this 1948 campaign button President Truman
wears an uncharacteristically blank expression.*

JUST PLAIN "S."

Harry S. Truman was introduced early to the political arts of compromise and persuasion. When he was born in 1884, his mother's family wanted his middle name to be Solomon, but the Trumans insisted on Shippe. His parents avoided choosing between the two old family names by making it "S.," pure and simple. As he grew up, Truman—by his own admission—made a habit of studying his teachers to see what pleased them and often became their pet. He watched everyone closely and "usually was able to get what [he] wanted." He learned, by reading history, that "a leader is a man who has the ability to get other people to do what they don't want to do, and like it." He had no idea how important that lesson would become.

Truman joined a Kansas City unit of the Missouri National Guard in 1905. When his unit was nationalized in World War I, he and a friend, Eddie Jacobson, were placed in charge of the regiment's canteen, which under their direction actually made a profit. Truman was shipped to France as an artillery officer (above), but after the war he and Jacobson got together again and went into business.

Childhood sweethearts, Harry Truman and Bess Wallace were in their thirties before they were finally married (above) in 1919. That fall Truman and Jacobson opened their ill-fated haberdashery in Kansas City. (Co-owner Truman is at far left in the photograph at left.) Truman could see only one reason for the shop's failure: "In 1921 . . . the Republicans took over. . . ." The store closed in 1922, when Truman was a candidate for district judge. (Below is one of his campaign buttons.) In 1935 he was sent to Washington as a senator.

Above, vice presidential candidate Truman confers with F. D. R. at the White House before the election of 1944. Below, the new Vice President, who loved to play the piano, performs for actress Lauren Bacall.

"YOU'D BE PRESIDENT"

During his first six years in the Senate, Truman's relationship with the notorious Kansas City political boss Tom Pendergast kept him out of the Roosevelt administration's inner circle. In his second term, however, his work as chairman of the Special Committee to Investigate the National Defense Program catapulted him to a position of respectability. As the national convention of 1944 approached, he was often mentioned as a possible vice presidential candidate. Told that F. D. R. would endorse him for the nomination, Truman replied, "Tell him to go to hell. I'm for Jimmy Byrnes." But the pressure was increased, and finally Truman gave in, accepted the challenge, and defeated Henry Wallace in the convention balloting. He had, however, made one mistake; he had forgotten to clear it with "the Boss"—Mrs. Truman. As they made their way from the convention floor to their car, she asked, "Are we going to have to go through this all the rest of our lives?" Truman said nothing. "What would happen," she demanded, "if he should die? You'd be President." If Truman answered at all, the reply was lost as their car sped away. Three months after the inauguration, F. D. R. did die. "I felt," Truman said, "like the moon, the stars, and all the planets had fallen on me. I've got the most terribly responsible job a man ever had."

At about 5 P.M. on April 12, 1945, a bored Harry S. Truman, presiding over the Senate, dashed off a letter to his mother and sister: "I am trying to write you . . . while a windy Senator . . . is making a speech on a subject with which he is in no way familiar. . . . Turn on your radio tomorrow night . . . you'll hear Harry make a Jefferson Day address to the nation. . . . It will be followed by the President, whom I'll introduce." He did not know it then, but Roosevelt had died. Truman took the oath of office (above) two hours later.

"A NEW WEAPON"

After he was sworn in, President Truman held a brief meeting with the grief-stricken Roosevelt Cabinet and asked its members to remain at their jobs. They agreed and solemnly departed, except for Secretary of War Henry L. Stimson. When he and Truman were alone, the Secretary told him that the United States had an atomic bomb; it was the first Truman heard of it. Originally intended for use against Germany, the bomb was not ready for testing until after V-E Day; and when the test was successfully concluded on the New Mexico desert in July, 1945, Truman was at Potsdam near Berlin, conferring with Winston Churchill and Joseph Stalin. The President and Prime Minister discussed the best way to tell Stalin about the bomb. Finally, Truman decided to mention casually that the United States now had "a new weapon of unusual destructive force." Stalin, according to Truman, replied that he was "glad to hear it and hoped we would make 'good use of it against the Japanese.'" Stalin was a good actor: his spy network had already informed him about the bomb.

The new Big Three at Potsdam (above) radiated good fellowship, harmony, and confidence. Actually, though Truman liked Stalin, Churchill disliked Truman, and Stalin distrusted both. Churchill was defeated in a British election before the conference at Potsdam ended and was replaced by Clement R. Attlee. At right is the mushroom cloud over Nagasaki, Japan, after an atomic bomb was dropped there on August 9, 1945.

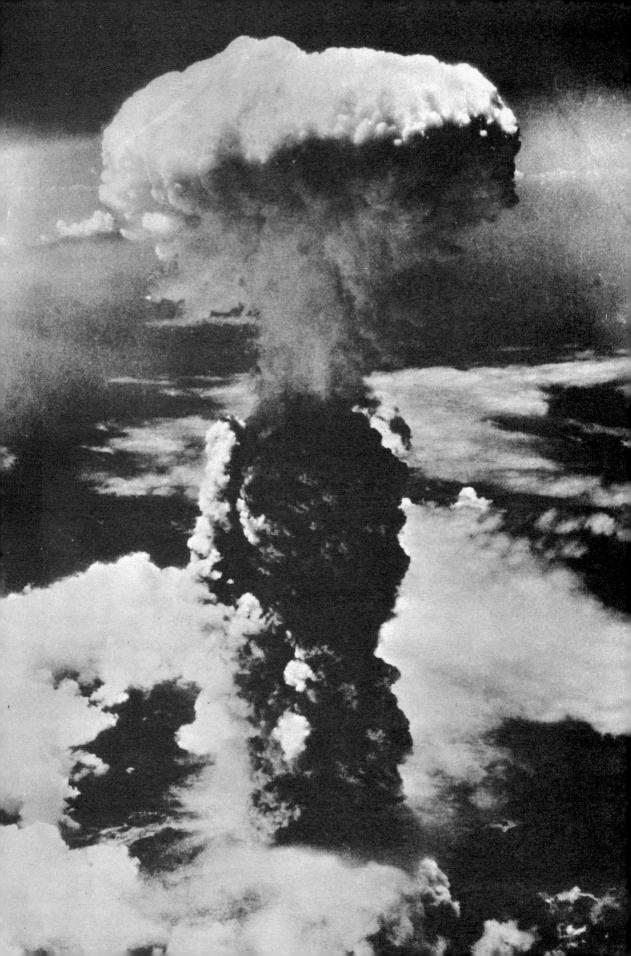

THE SCIENTISTS

NATIONAL PORTRAIT GALLERY SMITHSONIAN INSTITUTION

WIDE WORLD

ALBERT EINSTEIN

On August 2, 1939, the world-famous scientist Albert Einstein, alarmed at the progress of Nazi scientists in atomic research, wrote to President Roosevelt urging United States development of atomic weapons. His plea led to the creation of the atomic bomb six years later. Born in Ulm, Germany, in 1879, Einstein came to the world's attention in 1905 with his revolutionary theory that motion is not absolute but is relative to some fixed point of reference. In developing this special theory of relativity, he established the equivalence of mass and energy. It was his famous equation $E = MC^2$—a formula for the conversion of mass into energy—that made the atomic bomb possible. In subsequent research, Einstein expanded this concept in his general theory of relativity and opened new doors in the fields of gravitation, quantum theory, and the photoelectric effect of light. With the rise of Hitler in Germany, Einstein left Berlin and emigrated to America. Accepting a post at Princeton's Institute for Advanced Study in 1933, he remained there until his death in 1955, devoting his research to the formulation of a unified field theory. A gentle man with a penetrating sense of humor, Einstein—who won the Nobel Prize in 1921—once summed up his philosophy of life with this remark: "God is subtle, but he is not malicious."

ENRICO FERMI

In December, 1942, the beginning of the atomic age was announced by a coded telegram sent to Washington from the Chicago headquarters of the American atomic energy program: "The Italian navigator has entered the new world." The navigator referred to was Italian-born physicist Enrico Fermi, who had, in a nuclear reactor at the University of Chicago, just produced the first self-sustaining nuclear chain reaction in history. Fermi began experimenting with neutron bombardment in 1934, when he was a professor of physics at the University of Rome. While he narrowly missed discovering the secret of atomic fission himself, his work in the field led directly to that breakthrough and won him the Nobel Prize for physics in 1938. Leaving Fascist Italy, Fermi came to the United States in 1939 and became a professor at Columbia University. After the dramatic success of his nuclear reactor in 1942, he was transferred directly to the atomic bomb laboratory at Los Alamos. In 1946 he became a professor at the Institute of Nuclear Studies at Chicago, later renamed the Enrico Fermi Institute. Among his many contributions to physics were the Fermi-Dirac statistics of electron behavior, the theory of radioactive beta-ray disintegration, and the discovery of neptunium. He received the Special Award of the Atomic Energy Commission in 1954.

ERNEST ORLANDO LAWRENCE

The invention of the cyclotron by Ernest Orlando Lawrence was a giant step in the advancement of nuclear physics. Great strides had been made in the field of atomic research in the 1920's, but science had yet to produce a satisfactory device to penetrate the heart of the atom. In 1932 Lawrence, a professor of physics at the University of California, constructed the first such atom-smashing device—a circular, drum-shaped machine called a cyclotron. Within this device, atomic particles could be accelerated by repeated electrical charges to the extremely high velocities necessary to penetrate the nucleus of the atom, thereby causing atomic transmutation. After perfecting his cyclotron further, Lawrence proceeded with the systematic transmutation of all the atomic elements, and in 1936 he succeeded in the alchemist's dream of changing platinum into the next higher element, gold. That same year Lawrence was made director of the University of California Radiation Laboratory, and in 1939 he was awarded the Nobel Prize for his cyclotron. Using his invention to separate the highly fissionable uranium-235 from natural uranium, he was instrumental in the development of the atomic bomb during World War II. In 1957, the year before his death, Lawrence was the recipient of the Fermi Award of the Atomic Energy Commission.

JAMES B. CONANT

After the holocaust of World War II and the awesome demonstration of the atom's power to destroy, men of learning began to take a new look at the relationship of science to society. Scientist and educator James B. Conant, who had himself been instrumental in the production of the atomic bomb, was among those who later warned that "science alone, untempered by other knowledge, can lead not to freedom but to slavery." A graduate of Harvard, where he received a Ph.D. in 1916, Conant remained there as a chemistry professor, conducting important research in the field of organic chemistry. Appointed president of the university in 1933, he served in that position for twenty years. Chairman of the National Defense Research Committee from 1941 to 1946, Conant was a leading adviser in the government's atomic energy program, and after the war he helped to establish the National Science Foundation. Resigning from Harvard in 1953, he spent the next four years in West Germany as United States high commissioner and later as ambassador. Having recognized the need for "the interconnection of our new scientific knowledge and our older humanistic studies," Conant resumed his work in education under a Carnegie Foundation grant in 1957 and subsequently wrote a number of important books on education.

TRIALS AND
A NEW CRISIS

When President Truman said that he favored international trials for war criminals, he was severely criticized, and the Nuremberg Trials that resulted from his pressure are criticized to this day. What is forgotten, however, is that right after the war, critics of the plan did not oppose punishment—just trials. England, France, and Russia favored immediate executions without trials. But Truman, whose knowledge of history was extensive, was afraid that the horrible stories of Nazi concentration camps and of genocide would be regarded by later generations as "just a lot of propaganda." He wanted the films shown, the testimony recorded, and the Nazi directives read into a permanent document. He did not want Hitler to be remembered as a latter-day Napoleon. He wanted to set a precedent, to establish individual responsibility and punish guilty civilians along with the military. "Is it just . . ." he asked, "that the soldier who pulls the trigger or shovels the people into ovens shall be tried for murder . . . [while] the head of the government under whose activities and directives [he acts] shall be immune? . . . Now . . . nobody can say that it never happened, because the thing is on the record. Never again can men say, 'I was following orders.' And never again can men in power give such orders." The Nuremberg Trials were held, and their revelations shocked the world. Less than two years after they ended, Germany again became the focal point of world attention. Russia blocked off the autobahn to West Berlin in June, 1948, and a hot war was averted by the 321-day Berlin Airlift. Suddenly it became essential to have the support of the German people: the Russians, whose homeland had been ravaged by the Nazis, demanded East German support; the less-victimized, more-forgiving Americans simply wooed the West Germans and began the process of wiping the smeared slate clean.

Berlin, situated deep in the Soviet-occupied section of Germany, was divided into four sectors, each of which was controlled by one Allied power. But in 1948 the Russians closed the road that led through East Germany to Berlin. It was not the first hostile act of the cold war, but it was probably the one that firmly established the belligerence of the United States and the Soviet Union toward each other. President Truman responded by ordering supplies flown over East Germany to Berlin, daring the Russians to fire. At left, German workers unload fresh milk from an American plane. Below, children watch the arrival of a United States aircraft. The blockade, lifted in 1949, was a blunder: it made the Germans objects of sympathy. Inadvertently, the Russians had boosted West Germany onto the road to postwar recovery.

Friend of the People
HARRY S. TRUMAN

J. DOYLE DEWITT COLLECTION

At left and right are two souvenirs of the greatest up-
set in presidential election history, a Truman pen
and a premature newspaper. Below, Truman speaks
at a whistle-stop in Idaho—the kind of gathering
that forged the unexpected victory in 1948. It was
probably in the Farm Belt that his "give-'em-hell"
tactics worked best. Congress had not provided ade-
quate storage bins for the abundant crops. "When
you have to sell your grain below the support price
because you have no place to store it," Truman
harangued, "you can thank this same Republican
Congress." The farmers, who were enjoying their
greatest prosperity in thirty years, played safe and
stuck with President Truman and the Democrats.

"WHAT A LIFE!"

Had dinner by myself tonight . . ." Truman noted in 1949. "Barnett in tails and white tie pulls out my chair, pushes me up to the table. John in tails and white tie brings me a fruit cup, Barnett takes the empty cup. John brings me a plate, Barnett brings me a tenderloin. John brings me asparagus, Barnett brings me carrots and beets. . . . Barnett takes the plate and butter plates. John comes in with a napkin and silver crumb tray—there are no crumbs but John has to brush them off the table anyway. . . . Barnett brings me some chocolate custard. John brings me a demitasse (at home a little cup of coffee—about two good gulps) and my dinner is over. I take a hand bath in the finger bowl and go back to work. What a life!" Whatever Truman might have felt about the formality of presidential dining, he had fought the fight of his life to retain his job. No one—except himself—had thought he would remain in the White House. He had, a year before, run for re-election against a confident Thomas E. Dewey, and he had run with his own party divided, its left and right wings having bolted. But, on that 1949 evening, it was Harry Truman who responded when the butler said, "Mr. President, dinner is served."

931

MEN OF INFLUENCE

ARTHUR H. VANDENBERG

Senator Arthur H. Vandenberg's "long day's journey into our times" (in Dean Acheson's words) began in the heartland of isolationism. An influential Republican newspaper editor in his native Michigan, Vandenberg was appointed to fill a vacant Senate seat in 1928 and was subsequently elected to four full terms. He opposed lend-lease but altered his stance after the attack on Pearl Harbor, a day that "ended isolationism for any realist." His conversion to internationalism was gradual, however, and his support of Roosevelt's and of Truman's foreign policies was not unqualified—especially regarding some aspects of America's postwar involvement abroad. Acheson noted a certain "ritual of statesmanship" in Vandenberg's position on such projects as the United Nations Relief and Rehabilitation Administration and the Marshall Plan—first "opposition," then "gestation," and finally a demand for political concessions before giving his full and weighty stamp of approval. A delegate to the United Nations in 1945 and an adviser at the Paris conference of foreign ministers in 1946, Vandenberg became chairman of the Senate Committee on Foreign Affairs. He introduced a resolution stating America's "determination . . . to exercise the right of individual *or collective* self-defense," the basis for United States participation in NATO. Vandenberg died in office in 1951.

SAM RAYBURN

"They don't make them like that any more," was John F. Kennedy's apt remark as he left the bedside of a moribund Sam Rayburn in the fall of 1961. "Mr. Sam" was elected to the first of a record twenty-five consecutive congressional terms in 1912; he was Speaker of the House for seventeen years, more than doubling Henry Clay's tenure. Tennessee-born and Texas-raised, Rayburn knew poverty firsthand. His father told him, "Character is all I have to give you. Be a man." Rayburn worked his way through college and prepared for service on Capitol Hill with six years in the state legislature. Though a staunch Democrat, he was justly noted for his skill at persuasion and constructive compromise. In 1941 Congress was ready to kill the draft; Rayburn marshaled all his resources and saved it—by one vote—four months before Pearl Harbor. He led the postwar fight against isolationism, which could only "break the hearts of the world." Permanent chairman of three Democratic National Conventions, he was one of the most powerful men in government (he did some of his best politicking at informal "Rayburn Board of Education" sessions in his office). Once he was asked how he could remember all the promises he had made—or had refused to make. "If you tell the truth the first time," answered the Speaker of the House, "you don't have to remember."

DEAN ACHESON

In 1945 Under Secretary of State Dean Acheson said he had "no objective reason to suppose" that the vital interests of the United States and Russia would ever conflict. By 1949, just after he became head of the Department of State, he (along with millions of Americans) had changed his stance. He then saw communism as "economically fatal to free society and to human rights and fundamental freedoms." Over the next four years Acheson confirmed his commitment to this stiffer view. He helped create NATO and engineered the 1951 peace treaty with Japan; he supported the European Defense Community and implemented President Truman's policies in Korea. Acheson, who had attended Groton, Yale, and Harvard Law School, had been appointed under secretary of the treasury in 1933; opposed to F. D. R.'s gold-purchase plan, he was back in private practice inside of a year. In 1941, however, he became assistant secretary of state. He soon helped secure congressional passage of the lend-lease bill and, later, of the Bretton Woods Monetary Agreement. In 1946 he headed the committee that produced the Acheson-Lilienthal report, on which Bernard Baruch based his proposal for international control of atomic energy. Acheson returned to private practice in 1953; during the fifties he wrote a number of books on statecraft.

BERNARD M. BARUCH

"Most Presidents have received more advice than they can possibly use," wrote Harry S. Truman in his *Memoirs*. "But Baruch is the only man to my knowledge who has built a reputation on a self-assumed unofficial status as 'adviser.'" A millionaire at the age of thirty, financier Bernard M. Baruch left Wall Street in 1916 to advise President Wilson on national defense. He was chairman of the War Industries Board during World War I and later participated in the peace negotiations at Versailles. Between the world wars he helped to formulate policy on agriculture, neutrality, and defense, and in 1943 he was made special adviser to the Office of War Mobilization. In 1946 President Truman appointed him United States representative to the United Nations Atomic Energy Commission, in which capacity he presented the American plan for an international ban on atomic weapons. "We must elect World Peace or World Destruction," he warned in his opening statement. Russia's rejection of the plan was one of Baruch's greatest disappointments. "It took four years to win the war," wrote the aging statesman in 1960, "but in the fifteen years since, we have not yet been able to win the peace." Resigning from the commission in 1947, Baruch continued to serve the government in his capacity as an unofficial adviser. He died at ninety-five in June, 1965.

RENOVATIONS

White House social life under the close-knit Trumans was lively and informal and, thanks to Margaret's policy of being "at home" to all her school friends, youth oriented. In 1947, however, the Mansion's various creaks and tremblings and sagging second floor began to worry Truman, and when some beams gave way under the weight of Margaret's piano, he secured a congressional appropriation to thoroughly renovate the whole place. The President had an impressive knowledge of architecture and kept a close watch on all the reconstruction. While the work was being done the Trumans moved across the street to Blair House, where, in 1950, two Puerto Rican national-ists tried to kill the President. Truman was unhurt, but one Secret Service man and one would-be assassin were killed. The surviving gunner was sentenced to execution, but Truman commuted the sentence to life imprisonment. When the White House was ready for occupancy again, Margaret was around less; she had begun to try to build a career as a concert singer. When Truman was widely criticized for writing a blunt, bitter letter to a critic who had reviewed one of his daughter's performances harshly, the President wrote in his diary: "I'm accused of putting my baby who is the apple of my eye in a bad position. I don't think that is so. She doesn't either—thank the Almighty."

Blair House (above) was home for the Trumans for more than three years. From there the President took his famous morning strolls at a pace so quick that younger aides and reporters found it difficult to keep up.

With the White House being gutted and rebuilt (left), Mrs. Truman entertained guests in the Blair House sitting room (above).

Seated above is Alger Hiss, a State Department official who was convicted of perjury for denying old Communist ties. At right, Dean Acheson, with Truman and Alben Barkley, signs the NATO pact. Far right: victorious Chinese Communists in 1949.

SAUVONS LES ROSENBERG

GENEVIEVE

SPECIALITES POUR ENFANTS

MAGNUM/HENRI CARTIER BRESSON

WIDE WORLD

CONTAINMENT
AND HYSTERIA

World War II had been won because the Allies had subordinated their special interests to create unity. Capitalist and Communist, Chiang Kai-shek and Mao Tse-tung, Winston Churchill and Joseph Stalin, Greek monarchist and Greek rebel—all had fought together to break the back of the German, Italian, and Japanese aggressors. But postwar misunderstandings, naïveté, and distrust destroyed the inspiring unity quickly. As the Soviet sphere enlarged, as Mao and Chiang refused to cooperate and warred again, and as United States-Soviet Union relations deteriorated, the American people fidgeted. President Truman developed an effective containment policy, restricting Russian expansion and dealing with the Berlin blockade effectively, but the tension grew. Some voices in Congress began blaming the administration for all the tension—in effect, for all the world's troubles. Communist expansion, they said—wherever it occurred—was the result of "disloyalty" in American government. One of the nation's periodic witch hunts began. When Russia exploded an atomic bomb—its development had been facilitated by the treason of Klaus Fuchs in Britain and the Rosenbergs in the United States—and the Communists drove Chiang Kai-shek from the Chinese mainland, the hysteria at home worsened. It was, as one thing led to another and McCarthyism emerged, almost farcical: somebody knew someone who said so-and-so had married the sister of a French Communist, and soon so-and-so lost his job. Truman implored his countrymen not to "play it safe," not to hesitate to speak out on controversial issues. But playing it safe became the rule for many Americans for almost a decade.

At left, Parisians demonstrate vainly to save Ethel and Julius Rosenberg, convicted in 1951 of having given atomic secrets to Russia. They were the only American traitors ever executed in peacetime.

937

"THE GREATEST
LIVING AMERICAN"

I have no feelings," George Catlett Marshall told Dean Acheson in 1947, "except a few which I reserve for Mrs. Marshall." Joseph McCarthy agreed. Charging in 1951 that the general was a Communist-dominated traitor, the senator from Wisconsin asserted that Marshall "would sell his grandmother for any advantage." The charge, of course, was ridiculous. Despite his poor health, Marshall had been quietly serving his country for years while yearning for a retirement that America could not afford to let him have.

McCarthy's "man steeped in falsehood" had been promoted over thirty-four senior officers to the post of Army chief of staff by President Franklin D. Roosevelt, and he had been the principal military strategist for all Allied operations in Europe and the Pacific during World War II. The man who McCarthy said was party to "a conspiracy so immense and an infamy so black as to dwarf any previous venture in the history of man" was, after the war, immediately pressed into service by President Truman, who asked him to tackle the frustrating and hopeless job of trying to make peace between the warring Nationalist and Communist forces in China. The hard-working soldier turned statesman —whose activities as Truman's Secretary of State from 1947 to 1949, McCarthy held, were "invariably serving the world policy of the Kremlin"—helped the President to formulate the containment policy that halted Russian expansion and the Marshall Plan that revitalized Europe. As Secretary of Defense in 1950 and 1951, Marshall rebuilt the armed forces, equipping them to deal with Communist aggression during the Korean conflict.

Actually, both Marshall and McCarthy had lied. While Secretary of State, Marshall told Acheson, his major associate, that he had no feelings so that Acheson would not hesitate to criticize the State Department. McCarthy lied, political commentator Richard H. Rovere has written, to demonstrate that not even the most "unassailable" American was immune to his inquisition. He succeeded in muddying the chaste reputation of the man who Truman said was "the greatest living American."

Born in Uniontown, Pennsylvania, in 1880, Marshall began his Army career in 1901, after graduating from the Virginia Military Institute. Serving in the Philippines from 1913 to 1916, he was called by his commanding officer "the greatest military genius since Stonewall Jackson." During World War I he was instrumental in plotting the successful strategy of the St. Mihiel and Meuse-Argonne offensives. His administrative skills were bolstered by an extraordinary ability to recognize talent—one of the reasons why Roosevelt elevated him to the number one military position during World War II. It was General Marshall who recommended that Dwight D. Eisenhower be appointed— over three hundred and sixty-six senior officers—to command the United States forces in Europe.

In 1952, however, when Ike was running for the Presidency, he gave Marshall what was probably his most stinging slap in the face: Eisenhower refused to condemn McCarthy's assault on his old mentor. The retirement that Marshall had so long sought was finally his after Eisenhower's election. But both Eisenhower and the American people who had put up with the vilification of one of their greatest men were reminded of George Catlett Marshall's achievements when he was awarded the Nobel Prize for Peace in 1953, five years before his death.

George C. Marshall, painted by Thomas E. Stephens

MISCALCULATIONS

Early in 1950, when Secretary of State Dean Acheson defined the United States "defense perimeter" in the Far East, he excluded the Republic of South Korea. Korea, strategists had decided, was not worth defending. But in June, when troops from Communist North Korea crossed the thirty-eighth parallel and invaded the South, the strategists realized that they had miscalculated. It was probable that the North Koreans had been goaded by Red China, which was anxious to flex its international muscles. If Truman's containment policy was to mean anything, it would have to apply to Asia as well as to Europe. With the sanction of the United Nations, Truman appointed General Douglas MacArthur to command the United Nations troops (sixteen nations sent men, but 90 per cent of the soldiers were American). When the Chinese swarmed across the Yalu River in November —despite the general's repeated assurances that China would not enter the war—MacArthur diverted attention from his miscalculation by demanding permission to bomb China. Leaders of both the United States and the United Nations were certain that that would lead to World War III and refused. But MacArthur also miscalculated the nature of his chief, Harry Truman. The general continued to issue public statements and to write to sympathetic Republican congressmen. Ordered to refrain, he persisted, and Truman fired him. He came home to a hero's welcome and made a stirring speech to Congress. But the Constitution supported the President, and so did most military men. As General Omar Bradley testified, to attack China would have involved "us in the wrong war, at the wrong place, at the wrong time and with the wrong enemy."

Officially, the conflict in Korea was not a war; it was a "police action" by United Nations forces. At right, American soldiers cautiously search enemy huts for North Korean or Chinese guerrillas.

At their Wake Island meeting (above) in October, 1950, General Douglas MacArthur assured President Truman that Red China was not going to intervene in Korea. But on November 26, hordes of Chinese crossed the Yalu and swarmed over United Nations lines. Although the safe-conduct passes (below) dropped among enemy troops caused some defections, they had little effect on what MacArthur called the "bottomless well of Chinese manpower."

SAFE CONDUCT PASS

SOLDIERS OF THE UN FORCES:
This certificate guarantees good treatment to any enemy soldier desiring to cease fighting. Take this man to your nearest officer and treat him as an honorable prisoner of war.

Douglas MacArthur
DOUGLAS MacARTHUR
General of the Army
Commander-in-Chief

대한민국 병사에게
이것은 적의 군인으
로서 누구나 항복하기를
원한즉 자비게 인도하대
우를 봉종하는 증명서이다
이 사람을 가까이 있
는 당신의 상관에에 미
리 가지오. 이 사람을 면에
스로 포로로 대우하시오
백아 더장군 명령

TRUMAN'S ADVERSARIES

JOHN L. LEWIS

"He who tooteth not his own horn," said John Llewellyn Lewis, "the same shall not be tooted." And tooting his own horn—to a score that was often at great variance with the one being read by the conductor of the national orchestra—the labor leader with a flair for drama was a famous public figure during and after the New Deal. Born in Lucas, Iowa, in 1880, he became, at the age of seventeen, a coal miner, like his Welsh father. Lewis was a talented organizer and speaker; before he was thirty he was president of a United Mine Workers local in Illinois, and by 1920 he was head of the four-hundred-thousand-member national union. His leadership was at first conservative; he was a Republican, and the twenties were years of normalcy. The United Mine Workers shrank to about a quarter of its former size. But Lewis revitalized the union during the New Deal, and he and it became increasingly influential forces in national affairs. He tormented Presidents Roosevelt and Truman with defiance, sarcasm, and strike after strike, especially during World War II, which he seemed to view mainly as a chance to build union power. "Well, you have to admit," said F. D. R. (whose election Lewis had supported only once—in 1936), "Lewis has done a lot for the miners." Lewis, whose heavy eyebrows made him a favorite of cartoonists, retired in 1960.

HENRY WALLACE

During his twenty years in national politics Henry Wallace underwent a drastic ideological metamorphosis—and, finally, a dramatic reversal. Born in Iowa, he was a Republican and editor of the influential *Wallaces' Farmer* from 1924 until 1933, when F. D. R., whom he had supported, named him Secretary of Agriculture. Wallace supervised the controversial Agricultural Adjustment Administration, which hiked farm prices by a systematic destruction of produce. Conservative Democrats protested when F. D. R. chose him as the vice presidential candidate in 1940 ("Just because the Republicans have nominated an apostate Democrat," said one, "let us not for God's sake nominate an apostate Republican"), but Wallace was nominated and elected. In addition to making a number of wartime good-will tours, he headed two important economic bodies, but he had little influence with the Senate. He openly sympathized with Russia and was dropped from the ticket in 1944. Wallace then served as Secretary of Commerce but was dismissed for criticizing President Truman's "get tough" policy toward the U.S.S.R. Joining the Progressives, Wallace ran for the Presidency in 1948; four years later he published "Why I Was Wrong," an explanation of his new enmity toward Stalin's Soviet Union. An eminent plant geneticist, Wallace retired and turned to farming; he died in 1965.

J. STROM THURMOND

Senator J. Strom Thurmond of South Carolina was described by *Time* magazine as
"one of the Senate's deepest-dyed conserva-
tives and most colorful characters." A
former lawyer, state legislator, and circuit
judge, Thurmond was elected governor of
South Carolina on the Democratic ticket in
1946, and two years later ran for the Presidency as the candidate of the States' Rights
party. The governor's Southern followers,
popularly known as the Dixiecrats, had
bolted the Democratic party when its candidate, Harry S. Truman, had come out for
a strong civil rights platform. Unabashedly
opposing any program of "social equality
by Federal fiat," Thurmond captured four
Southern states and received a popular vote
of 1,169,063. Entering the United States
Senate as a Democrat in 1955, he set a fili-
buster record two years later in a one-man
battle against civil rights legislation. In 1962
he set off a congressional investigation with
charges that the State Department was
"muzzling" the military, which alone had
a real "understanding of the Communist
threat." Having gone about as far right as
possible within the Democratic party, Senator Thurmond supported Barry Goldwater
for the Presidency in 1964. Firmly ensconced
in the Republican right wing, he remained,
as the *New Republic* commented in 1965, "a
determined defender of lost causes. . . ."

DOUGLAS MacARTHUR

When Douglas MacArthur promised to return to the Philippines after the Japanese
had forced him to retreat in 1942, he was
displaying both the dedicated courage that
made him an effective general and the ego-
centricity that his critics decried. The top
scholar in the West Point class of 1903,
MacArthur had served first in the Far East
and had then participated valiantly in the
Meuse-Argonne campaign of World War I.
After three years as superintendent at West
Point and further service in the Far East, he
became a full general. In 1930 he was named
Army chief of staff. MacArthur retired in
1937 but was recalled in 1941 to head the
Far East command. In May, 1942, his
forces began the long drive to retake the
Philippines—and in October, 1944, the gen-
eral, true to his word, waded ashore at
Leyte. Awarded a fifth star in 1944, he re-
ceived Japan's surrender on September 2,
1945. He then oversaw the occupation of
Japan and in 1950 took command of the
United Nations forces in Korea. Because
MacArthur publicly criticized American and
United Nations policies in Korea, Truman
relieved him of command in 1951. Accorded
a hero's welcome by the American people,
he was considered a presidential prospect,
but the Republicans chose Eisenhower.
MacArthur became chairman of Remington
Rand, Incorporated, and died in 1964.

RESPONSIBILITIES

In retirement, Harry Truman often acted the curmudgeon—perhaps to conceal the fact that he was becoming a mellow old gentleman who genuinely liked people. Journalist Eric Sevareid discovered in 1964 that there was a side to Truman that was seldom noticed. "We were aware," he wrote, "of his sensitivity about the institution of the presidency . . . [and] lack of sensitivity to criticism of himself.

MAGNUM/ELLIOTT ERWITT

Back home in Independence, Truman (above) set up a library, wrote his memoirs, answered mail, and dismissed suggestions that he had been a great President. In 1961 he visited Washington and played the piano for John F. Kennedy and his guests (right).

What we were not aware of . . . was his sensitivity about the feelings of other people." Once, Sevareid elaborated, Truman, who was speaking to a college audience, had admonished a student for referring to the governor of the state as a "local yokel." Instantly Truman "realized how a public scolding by a former President could mark and mar the boy's inner life and his standing in the community." So he sought out the boy, re-assured him, and followed, as a friend, his scholastic progress and later career. Truman's kindness gave Sevareid "an insight to the responsibilities of a President that I did not have, and it has immeasurably added to my own residue of memories about the man from Missouri. . . . He may live to be 100—his is strong stock—but this, I know, is the specific memory that will return to me when his time does come."

FACTS IN SUMMARY: HARRY S. TRUMAN

CHRONOLOGY

UNITED STATES		TRUMAN
Cleveland elected President	1884	*Born May 8*
Sherman Antitrust Act	1890	*Moves to Independence*
Cleveland re-elected	1892	*Enters elementary school*
War with Spain	1898	
McKinley assassinated	1901	*Graduates from high school*
Theodore Roosevelt becomes President		*Works as timekeeper for railroad*
	1902	*Works for Kansas City Star*
Elkins Act	1903	*Becomes bank clerk in Kansas City*
	1905	*Joins Missouri National Guard*
Pure Food and Drug Act	1906	*Works on father's farm*
Wilson elected President	1912	
War with Germany	1917	*Elected first lieutenant in National Guard regiment*
Battle of Belleau Wood	1918	*Commands Battery D, 129th Field Artillery, with rank of captain*
Second Battle of the Marne		*Fights at St. Mihiel, Meuse-Argonne, Sommedieu*
World War I ends		
Eighteenth Amendment ratified	1919	*Marries Bess Wallace*
		Opens haberdashery
Capper-Volstead Act	1922	*Elected judge of county court for Eastern District, Jackson County, Mo.*
	1924	*Loses bid for re-election*
	1926	*Elected presiding judge of county court, Jackson County, Mo.*
Hoover elected President	1928	
Stock market crash	1929	
Roosevelt elected President	1932	
New Deal measures	1933	
National Labor Relations Board created	1934	*Elected to U.S. Senate*
Works Progress Administration created	1935	
Social Security established		
Roosevelt re-elected	1936	
Roosevelt attempts to increase Supreme Court membership	1937	
World War II begins in Europe	1939	
Roosevelt re-elected	1940	*Re-elected to Senate*
Pearl Harbor bombed	1941	*Appointed chairman of Senate Committee to Investigate the National Defense Program*
U.S. declares war on Japan		
Battle of Midway	1942	
Allies invade Italy	1943	
Allied invasion of Normandy	1944	*Elected Vice President*
Roosevelt re-elected		
Roosevelt dies	1945	*Becomes President*
Germany surrenders		*Attends Potsdam Conference*
United Nations Charter signed		*Orders A-bombs dropped on Japan*
Atomic bombs dropped on Hiroshima and Nagasaki		*Appoints Nuremberg Trials justices*
Japan surrenders		
Atomic Energy Commission established	1946	*Recommends statehood for Alaska and Hawaii*
Paris Peace Conference		*Seizes railroads and coal mines*
		Proclaims Philippine independence
Taft-Hartley Act passed over presidential veto	1947	*Issues Truman Doctrine*
		Establishes Marshall Plan
Berlin Airlift	1948	*Elected President*
NATO pact signed	1949	*Formulates Point Four program*
Korean War begins	1950	*Sends U.S. troops to Korea to repel Communist invasion*
U.N. sanctions U.S. action in Korea		*Vetoes Internal Security Act*
Internal Security Act passed over veto		
Japanese Peace Treaty signed	1951	*Relieves MacArthur of Far East command*
Eisenhower elected President	1952	*Seizes steel mills to prevent strike*
Supreme Court declares seizure of steel mills illegal		*Warns against danger of McCarthyism*
Bricker amendment		
Eisenhower inaugurated	1953	*Retires to Independence*
Korean War armistice		
Eisenhower re-elected	1956	*Publishes memoirs*
Federal troops sent to Little Rock, Ark.	1957	*Presents Truman Library to National Archives*
Kennedy elected President	1960	*Supports Stuart Symington for presidential nomination*
Kennedy assassinated	1963	
Johnson becomes President		
Intensification of war in Vietnam	1966	

BIOGRAPHICAL FACTS

BIRTH: Lamar, Mo., May 8, 1884

ANCESTRY: Scotch-English

FATHER: John Anderson Truman; b. Jackson County, Mo., Dec. 5, 1851; d. Grandview, Mo., Nov. 3, 1914

FATHER'S OCCUPATION: Farmer

MOTHER: Martha Ellen Young Truman; b. Jackson County, Mo., Nov. 25, 1852; d. Grandview, Mo., July 26, 1947

BROTHER: Vivian (1886–1965)

SISTER: Mary Jane (1889–   )

WIFE: Elizabeth Virginia Wallace; b. Independence, Mo., Feb. 13, 1885

MARRIAGE: Independence, Mo., June 28, 1919

CHILD: Margaret (1924–   )

EDUCATION: Graduated from public high school

RELIGIOUS AFFILIATION: Baptist

OCCUPATIONS BEFORE PRESIDENCY: Railroad timekeeper; bank clerk; farmer; haberdasher

MILITARY SERVICE: Missouri National Guard; captain in 129th Field Artillery (1918–1919)

PRE-PRESIDENTIAL OFFICES: County Judge for Eastern District of Jackson County, Mo.; Presiding Judge, County Court, Jackson County, Mo.; United States Senator; Vice President

AGE AT INAUGURATION: 60

OCCUPATION AFTER PRESIDENCY: Writer

FIRST ADMINISTRATION

INAUGURATION: April 12, 1945; the White House, Washington, D.C.

SECRETARY OF STATE: Edward R. Stettinius; James F. Byrnes (from July 3, 1945); George C. Marshall (from Jan. 21, 1947)

SECRETARY OF THE TREASURY: Henry Morgenthau, Jr.; Fred M. Vinson (from July 23, 1945); John W. Snyder (from June 25, 1946)

SECRETARY OF DEFENSE (Department created in September, 1947): James V. Forrestal

SECRETARY OF WAR: Henry L. Stimson; Robert P. Patterson (from Sept. 27, 1945); Kenneth C. Royall (from July 25, 1947—Department disbanded in September, 1947)

ATTORNEY GENERAL: Francis Biddle; Thomas C. Clark (from July 1, 1945)

POSTMASTER GENERAL: Frank C. Walker; Robert E. Hannegan (from July 1, 1945); Jesse M. Donaldson (from Dec. 16, 1947)

SECRETARY OF THE NAVY: James V. Forrestal (Department disbanded in September, 1947)

SECRETARY OF THE INTERIOR: Harold L. Ickes; Julius A. Krug (from March 18, 1946)

SECRETARY OF AGRICULTURE: Claude R. Wickard; Clinton P. Anderson (from June 30, 1945); Charles F. Brannan (from June 2, 1948)

SECRETARY OF COMMERCE: Henry A. Wallace; W. Averell Harriman (from Jan. 28, 1947); Charles Sawyer (from May 6, 1948)

SECRETARY OF LABOR: Frances Perkins; Lewis B. Schwellenbach (from July 1, 1945); Maurice J. Tobin (from Aug. 13, 1948)

SUPREME COURT APPOINTMENTS: Harold H. Burton (1945); Fred M. Vinson, Chief Justice (1946)

79th CONGRESS (January 3, 1945–January 3, 1947):
Senate: 56 Democrats; 38 Republicans; 1 Other
House: 242 Democrats; 190 Republicans; 2 Others

80th CONGRESS (January 3, 1947–January 3, 1949):
Senate: 51 Republicans; 45 Democrats
House: 245 Republicans; 188 Democrats; 1 Other

ELECTION OF 1948

CANDIDATES	ELECTORAL VOTE	POPULAR VOTE
Harry S. Truman Democratic	303	24,105,812
Thomas E. Dewey Republican	189	21,970,065
Strom Thurmond States' Rights	39	1,169,063
Henry Wallace Progressive	—	1,157,172
Norman Thomas Socialist	—	139,414
Claude A. Watson Prohibition	—	103,224

SECOND ADMINISTRATION

INAUGURATION: January 20, 1949; the Capitol, Washington, D.C.

VICE PRESIDENT: Alben W. Barkley

SECRETARY OF STATE: Dean G. Acheson

SECRETARY OF THE TREASURY: John W. Snyder

SECRETARY OF DEFENSE: James V. Forrestal; Louis A. Johnson (from March 28, 1949); George C. Marshall (from Sept. 21, 1950); Robert A. Lovett (from Sept. 17, 1951)

ATTORNEY GENERAL: Thomas C. Clark; J. Howard McGrath (from Aug. 24, 1949); James P. McGranery (from May 27, 1952)

POSTMASTER GENERAL: Jesse M. Donaldson

SECRETARY OF THE INTERIOR: Julius A. Krug; Oscar L. Chapman (from Jan. 19, 1950)

SECRETARY OF AGRICULTURE: Charles F. Brannan

SECRETARY OF COMMERCE: Charles Sawyer

SECRETARY OF LABOR: Maurice J. Tobin

SUPREME COURT APPOINTMENTS: Thomas C. Clark (1949); Sherman Minton (1949)

81st CONGRESS (January 3, 1949–January 3, 1951):
Senate: 54 Democrats; 42 Republicans
House: 263 Democrats; 171 Republicans; 1 Other

82nd CONGRESS (January 3, 1951–January 3, 1953):
Senate: 49 Democrats; 47 Republicans
House: 234 Democrats; 199 Republicans; 1 Other

Mr. Lessing J. Rosenwald
Jenkintown
Pennsylvania

THE THIRTY-FOURTH PRESIDENT (1953–1961)

DWIGHT DAVID EISENHOWER

On June 23, 1942, a little-known fifty-one-year-old major general boarded a London-bound plane in Washington, D.C. He had recently been appointed to command the European Theater of Operations—ETO, the new military organization that formally signaled America's entry into the fight against Nazi Germany. Newspapermen who had done their homework had learned only that the officer was generally regarded as a technical expert, that he was genial and was well liked by his colleagues, and that his friends called him Ike.

So limited was the reputation of Dwight David Eisenhower in 1942 that he might well have been considered a secret weapon. But Great Britain, unimpressed by Ike's appointment, was given no reason to hold such a romantic hope. Except for the British Isles, Russia, and several neutral, or nominally neutral, nations, all Europe belonged to Hitler's Third Reich. To the east, the Russians had stopped the Germans before they reached Moscow, but the winter was over and the Germans were still deep in Soviet territory. To the south, on the sands of North Africa, English troops reeled under successive defeats administered by General Erwin Rommel; two days after Eisenhower arrived in London, Rommel crossed the border into Egypt. It could hardly escape the attention of the British that the man America had sent to reverse the course of the war was one whose military career was known only through the official mimeographed biography handed out by the United States War Department.

Eisenhower had graduated from West Point (at the bottom edge of the top third of his class) in 1915. During World War I he had commanded a tank-training school at Camp Colt, near Gettysburg, Pennsylvania. By the time he had turned twenty-seven, he had had some six thousand men under his

President Eisenhower in 1956

Dwight, extreme left, was about ten when the family sat for this portrait. Between David and Ida Eisenhower is Milton—with curls; Earl and Roy are to Ike's left in the second row; at top are Edgar and Arthur.

command and had become noted for his administrative ability.

From 1922 to 1924 he had served in the Panama Canal Zone as an executive officer for Brigadier General Fox Connor, who had compared Eisenhower favorably with a young major named George C. Marshall and had inspired Ike to continue studying strategy and the history of warfare. (Eisenhower had always been interested in those subjects. He had read about Hannibal during his high-school years, had analyzed the mistakes of the British as he had wandered over Revolutionary War battle sites near West Point while a student there, and had digested the lessons of the Battle of Gettysburg when he had been at Camp Colt.)

In 1925 Eisenhower entered the Command and General Staff School. Although he had previously been an average student, he graduated first in a class of two hundred and seventy-five, having been able to cope with the competitive pressures that drove other Command students to exhaustion, retirement, and even nervous breakdowns and suicide. In 1927 Ike was assigned to write a guide to the European battlefields of

World War I. It remains one of the best works on the war and is—in view of Eisenhower's syntax as President—remarkably articulate. From 1929 to 1932 he served as an assistant executive to the assistant secretary of war, and was then assigned to the staff of General Douglas MacArthur, the Army chief of staff, in Washington. From 1935 until Hitler attacked Poland in 1939, he was General MacArthur's assistant in the Philippines. Subsequently Eisenhower was assigned to various posts within the United States.

In September of 1941, in order to test the new Army the United States was training for the impending war, a mock battle was staged in Louisiana. Eisenhower was named chief of staff for the Third Army, which fought and won two battles against the Second Army. He had learned about tanks during World War I, he had learned to fly a plane in the Philippines, and he had always believed that mastery of these two weapons would determine the victor in any future war. It was the precise coordination between tanks and planes that won the battles in Louisiana. Two days after the victory,

Ike once figured out that the house in Abilene had 818 square feet (including this parlor); there were eight in the family, and his mother "not only managed to fit us all in, she used the space beautifully."

Eisenhower was promoted to the temporary rank of brigadier general.

Shortly after the attack on Pearl Harbor, Eisenhower was called to Washington to serve as an assistant chief of staff to George C. Marshall. He helped draft a global strategy for the war, followed this up with an outline for a cross-Channel invasion of the Continent, designed the ETO command that would carry out the strategies, and then boarded the plane to London.

His career seemed to have been respectable but not especially brilliant. Looking for some factor that might have accounted for Ike's appointment to the monumental ETO job, the journalists turned to his private life. Eisenhower, one of six sons of David and Ida Elizabeth Stover Eisenhower, had been born in Denison, Texas, on October 14, 1890. (A seventh son had died in early childhood.) When he was still an infant, his family moved to Abilene, Kansas, where he lived until he went to West Point. Ike's father, a mechanic in an Abilene creamery, held weekly Bible reading sessions; his mother was a Fundamentalist—and a pacifist. Although the sons were never religious, they

did absorb a profound belief in honesty and justice.

At the time of Eisenhower's birth, Abilene was only beginning to transform itself from a frontier cow town into a modern city of paved streets, sewers, streetcars, and telephones. The railroad tracks separated the well-to-do and the poor sections of town; Eisenhower lived on the wrong side of the tracks. There was a traditional rivalry between the boys who lived in the two sections, and every year a representative from each side met in a fist fight. When Eisenhower was fifteen, he engaged a boy named Wes Merrifield in such a contest. Merrifield was bigger and quicker, and the town's boys believed that Eisenhower would be knocked out in no time at all. After two full hours of fighting, however, Merrifield announced that he could not beat Eisenhower. Refusing to say that he could not beat Merrifield, Eisenhower reportedly admitted, "Well, Wes, I *haven't* licked you."

A few months after his fight with Merrifield, Eisenhower fell and skinned a knee. Blood poisoning developed and spread through his entire leg, and the doctor insisted that amputation was necessary. According to a biographer, Kenneth S. Davis, Eisenhower told his brother Edgar to stand guard at his bed to prevent the doctor from operating: "You got to promise me you won't let 'em do it," he sobbed. "You got to promise. I won't be a cripple. I'd rather die." For two days and nights, Edgar stood by as the doctor warned David and Ida Eisenhower that Ike might die. When the infection subsided, the lesson was not lost on Eisenhower: sheer will was a strong weapon.

Although the sport most commonly associated with Eisenhower is golf, football was his favorite. At first he played in the line and then switched to left half at West Point. While tackling Jim Thorpe, he wrenched a knee and a week later broke the knee in another game. He never played again. (His friends at West Point would say later that they thought his inability to play football

was the greatest disappointment of his life.) Football is a sport of exacting teamwork—and "teamwork" and "cooperation" are two words that occur very often in Dwight Eisenhower's speeches and writings as general and President.

All the Eisenhower boys were expected to help support the family. As youngsters, they took the produce grown in their garden, put it in a wagon, and sold it on the north side of town. Later Eisenhower worked in the Abilene creamery, where he met Everett "Swede" Hazlett, Jr., a young man who had managed to earn an appointment to the United States Naval Academy. Swede suggested that it would be fun if Eisenhower joined him at Annapolis. Eisenhower agreed, and took the examinations for both Annapolis and West Point. It was, of course, West Point to which he was appointed.

Reporters who wrote about Eisenhower in June, 1942, were able to add that in the autumn of 1915, two weeks after he was posted to Fort Sam Houston in San Antonio, Texas, he met and courted Mamie Doud, a strikingly pretty brunette socialite from Denver. Four months later they became engaged, and on July 1, 1916, they were married. Their first son, born in 1917, died in 1921; a second boy, John, was born in 1922.

That first impressions count is attested to by Eisenhower's career. In 1942 the journalists created an image that has not changed materially. They found him to be likable, modest, kindly, and a good administrator—brilliant, if at all, only in tactical matters. Failing to discover anything about him that portended greatness, they portrayed him as a good man.

Of Eisenhower's command in World War II, little needs to be said. He led the invasions of North Africa, Sicily, and the Italian mainland, the cross-Channel invasion of France, and the defeat of the German armies beyond the Rhine. It has often been remarked that he was not a general but an

In April of 1945, Generals Bradley, Patton, and Eisenhower, left to right, inspected art treasures stolen by the Nazis and cached in German salt mines.

In 1948 Secretary of Defense Forrestal sought the military views of the head of Columbia University.

administrator, not a strategist but a super-executive, not a great commander but a public relations expert who put over the biggest campaign of them all. But Eisenhower's role should not be underestimated. Although he was not a dashing, colorful general like Douglas MacArthur, it seems highly unlikely that a MacArthur, with all his bravura, could have welded together, as Eisenhower did, the Allied forces into a smooth, efficient war machine.

Eisenhower emerged from the war as the famous Ike, the military hero with the infectious grin who had led the troops to victory, and the personification of the good American who had overcome evil.

In Berlin in 1945, Eisenhower later wrote in *Mandate for Change*, "President Truman, riding with General Bradley and me . . . abruptly said that he would help me get anything I might want, including the Presidency in 1948." Eisenhower laughed and continued to laugh at such propositions for several years. After the war, he served as chief of staff, overseeing the demobilization of the American forces, a task he found "frankly distasteful."

As suggestions that he run for President became more persistent, Eisenhower noted that his "sense of humor was beginning to show signs of wear and tear." In 1948, just before the primaries, he wrote his famous letter to a newspaper publisher in New Hampshire, in which he stated that "the necessary and wise subordination of the military to civil power will be best sustained . . . when lifelong professional soldiers, in the absence of some obvious and overriding reasons, abstain from seeking high political office." Politics, he said, "is a profession; a serious, complicated, and, in its true sense, a noble one. . . . nothing in the international or domestic situation especially qualifies for the most important office in the world a man whose adult years have been spent in the country's military forces." It was a remarkable statement of principle from a military man—and, of course, it only made him more desirable to the electorate.

Also in 1948, Eisenhower's war memoirs, *Crusade in Europe*, were published, and they added to his fame and popularity. He served for two years as president of Columbia University in New York City, and was recalled to the Army in 1950 by President Truman to head the creation of military forces for the North Atlantic Treaty Organization, a job he completed with dispatch.

It may well have been the Korean War that placed Eisenhower in the Presidency. He deeply felt, as he had said and written, that the freedom won in World War II should be preserved and a better world created. His feelings coincided with those of most Americans. When in the fall of 1950 Chinese troops entered the Korean War and pushed the forces of the United Nations south of the thirty-eighth parallel, it seemed that all the gains won in the bloody years of World War II were to be lost. "At best," as Eisenhower wrote, "the prospects in Korea appeared to be for an eventual stalemate; at worst they boded . . . the beginning of World War III." Americans turned to the man who embodied the triumph of the last war; simply to place him in America's highest office seemed to reaffirm the permanence of its hard-fought-for values. In retrospect, political writers have tended to denigrate the voters' wish for a "father image," the need for "security." But the need was profound, and it was one to which Eisenhower—whether he possessed ambitions or not—could not fail to respond.

Once he had committed himself to the Presidency, his campaign was less a contest than a prolonged triumphal parade. He had repeatedly said that he had never been a political animal. There was, in fact, some question as to whether Eisenhower was a Republican or a Democrat. He permitted Senator Henry Cabot Lodge to announce that he was a Republican and promptly took the Republican nomination from Senator Robert A. Taft on the first ballot at the 1952 convention. The campaign was disappointing. Eisenhower remained genial but aloof, declining to engage in telling debate with his opponent, the witty and urbane Adlai Stevenson. Eisenhower spoke of the evil of Communist infiltration in the government, of corruption in Washington, and of the need to end the Korean War. He confined himself to lofty ideals: freedom in America and in the world; individualism and self-reliance; compassion for the weaker and less fortunate.

The most embarrassing moment in the campaign occurred when his running mate, Richard Nixon, had the charge of corruption turned against him. He was accused of having accepted a substantial sum of money from businessmen to finance his career. The episode was doubly embarrassing not because the accusation was true but because Nixon chose to tearfully defend himself, flanked by his wife, and his dog, Checkers, on nationwide television.

Eisenhower remained aloof from the controversy surrounding Senator Joseph R. McCarthy and from McCarthy's charge that Eisenhower's old friend and mentor, General Marshall, had been a pawn of the Communists. When Eisenhower declined to give McCarthy a roasting for the attack, and when he publicly embraced Senator William Jenner of Indiana, who had called Marshall "a living lie," he was severely criticized. He chose to wait, he told his friends, until McCarthy destroyed himself, insisting that it was

McCarthyism, not McCarthy, that needed destroying—and that only McCarthy himself could destroy McCarthyism. It was a neat explanation, but Eisenhower always tried to shun difficult, emotion-charged situations. During the war, he had insisted that his officers argue out their differences of opinion among themselves rather than bring them to him.

His most successful campaign maneuver was his promise to go to Korea and end the war there if elected. The promise clinched what was probably already a certain victory. He carried all but nine states, trouncing Stevenson with a plurality of more than six million votes.

In his book *The Effective Executive*, Peter F. Drucker remarked that a perfectly efficient executive nearly always ends up by creating a tedious organization. Eisenhower, "the Great Delegator," came close to being a tedious administrator—and would have been, had not several of his aides turned out to be unpredictable.

He made his political liaison man, former New Hampshire Governor Sherman Adams, assistant to the President and gave him Cabinet rank. Eisenhower's critics have maintained that he surrendered too much of his power to Adams; Eisenhower, however, clearly felt that domestic politics required a Cabinet official in the same way that foreign affairs required a Secretary of State. His mistake was openly delegating great power to Adams. There was little grief when the latter finally tendered his resignation after it was discovered that he had accepted favors (including the famous vicuna coat) from a New England industrialist.

The most diverting man in Eisenhower's Cabinet was Charles E. Wilson, the Secretary of Defense. As the president of General Motors Corporation, he had accumulated several millions of dollars worth of General Motors stock and expected to receive cash and stock bonuses for four more years. In reviewing his appointment to the Cabinet, the Senate wondered aloud whether Wilson might be inclined to favor General Motors in government contracts because of his conflict of interest. "For years," Wilson replied, "I thought what was good for the country was good for General Motors and vice versa." Though Wilson was finally persuaded to divest himself of his stock, political pundits mocked him for years thereafter. In the hands of cartoonist Al Capp, his statement became a belligerent, self-satisfied "What's good for General Bullmoose is good for the country." With the help of Admiral Arthur W. Radford, chairman of the joint chiefs of staff, Wilson did a creditable job, unifying the armed forces and making them into a defense establishment capable of effecting the much-criticized policy of massive retaliation. He managed, too, to call the members of the National Guard a bunch of "draft dodgers" and to characterize the Suez Crisis as a mere "ripple." Although he may have been right, Wilson was an embarrassment to the administration and finally resigned at the beginning of President Eisenhower's second term.

The globe-trotting and moralistic John Foster Dulles, Eisenhower's Secretary of State, stated the most chilling of all cold-war policies in a *Life* magazine article in 1956: "The ability to get to the verge [of war] without getting into the war is the necessary art. . . . If you are scared to go to the brink, you are lost. We've had to look it square in the face—on the question of enlarging the Korean war, on the question of getting into the Indochina war, on the question of Formosa. We walked to the brink and we looked it in the face."

This was brinkmanship. It was in this context of "thinking about the unthinkable" that Herman Kahn was led to write *On Thermonuclear War*, which embraced the notion that one day Russia and the United States could trade the annihilation of Moscow for that of New York in a war lasting several minutes. It is some measure of the impact brinkmanship had on many Americans that some critics could greet Kahn as a moderate.

On July 26, 1953, a few months after Eisenhower took office, the Korean War was ended by armistice. It cannot be said that

Mamie's 1953 inaugural-ball gown was embroidered with over two thousand stones—all sewed on by hand.

Eisenhower ended the war, as he had promised in his campaign. The North Koreans and Chinese had already decided to stop fighting. It can be said, however, that Eisenhower resisted any temptation to move into North Korea, as South Korea's President Syngman Rhee was so anxious to do. In April, after the Communists had offered to resume peace talks, Rhee had written Eisenhower that South Korea would continue to fight. When Eisenhower scotched that idea, the Communists and the United Nations forces agreed on voluntary repatriation of prisoners of war—the greatest stumbling block in negotiations to that point—and began to discuss a cease-fire line. Then Rhee permitted twenty-five thousand anti-Communist North Korean prisoners to escape, and Eisenhower found it necessary in a press conference to remind a reporter: "The enemy is still in *North* Korea." A scorching letter to Rhee and the visit of a State Department aide finally brought forth Rhee's public promise to abide by an armistice—and the war was ended.

In *The Cold War As History*, Louis J. Halle called Dulles a "hard" and Eisenhower a "soft" in the Russian-American contest. Whereas Eisenhower worked tirelessly to reduce tensions between the two nations, Dulles, in his public utterances and diplomatic maneuvers, tended to draw the line separating the two nations more sharply. Ultimately, Eisenhower's attitudes can be said to have won out, but not before the fight against what was identified as a monolithic communism was carried into Asia. American money financed in large part the French struggle against Communists in Vietnam, and it was with great reluctance that Eisenhower declined to send troops to aid the French at Dienbienphu. Shortly after the French forces were defeated in 1954, the Southeast Asia Treaty Organization (SEATO) was established. The United States pledged that any armed attack against a member nation in Southeast Asia (including South Vietnam) "would endanger its own peace and safety." The treaty was one more extension of America's commitment to keep the peace;

by the time Eisenhower left office in 1961, that commitment had been extended to cover most of the earth.

On April 22, 1954, after many years of wrangling over false charges of subversion in the military forces, Joseph McCarthy was taken to task by his strongest opponent, the United States Army. Charles Wilson characterized McCarthy's attacks on the Army as "just damn tommyrot." Senator Ralph Flanders of Vermont remarked on the Senate floor: "He dons his war paint. He goes into his war dance. He emits his war whoops. He goes forth to battle and proudly returns with the scalp of a pink Army dentist. We may assume that this represents the depth of the seriousness of Communist penetration at this time."

The Army seized upon its own notion of a serious charge—that McCarthy's aide Roy M. Cohn had demanded special treatment for his former associate Private G. David Schine, under the threat that Cohn would "wreck the Army" if not satisfied. For a period of more than fifty days, the Army proceeded to wreck McCarthy in televised hearings in which doctored photographs were revealed, points of order were made, and, finally, as Eisenhower wrote, "a near fist fight [broke out] between Roy Cohn and the counsel for Democratic members of the subcom-

The public was kept well informed of Eisenhower's progress during the medical crises of his two terms. Here the Walter Reed Hospital commandant, General Leonard Heaton, explains Ike's ileitis operation of 1956.

mittee." Eisenhower himself remained aloof from the proceedings, arguing (he was considerably more justified this time than he had been in his explanation for avoiding condemnation of McCarthy during the campaign) that the President should not wage war on a member of the legislature. McCarthy was condemned by the Senate on December 2 and died a broken and pathetic man three years later.

On May 17, 1954, the Supreme Court handed down its epochal decision that racial segregation in public schools was unconstitutional. It was with that decision that students began to march, picket, and riot for civil rights. Eisenhower had always been committed to "equality before the law of all citizens. . . ." To civil rights leaders, however, his response to the Supreme Court decision seemed minimal. Not until Governor Orval Faubus of Arkansas called out National Guard troops to prevent Negro students from entering Central High School in Little Rock in September, 1957, did Eisenhower act firmly. On only thirteen previous occasions had a President dispatched federal troops into a state to enforce federal law. But after rioting broke out in Little Rock, Eisenhower sent in one thousand paratroopers and federalized more than ten thousand National Guardsmen. Nothing of consequence was accomplished in Little Rock itself. But four days before Governor Faubus called out the National Guard, the first civil rights bill to pass Congress since 1875 had been approved, with President Eisenhower's blessing, authorizing a Civil Rights Commission. Civil rights, the most painful domestic problem, was brought into the open.

Although much of his foreign policy during his first four years solidified the hostility between America and Russia, Eisenhower nonetheless worked at reducing the tension. In one of his first speeches as President (to the American Society of Newspaper Editors on April 16, 1953), Eisenhower had said: "Every gun that is made, every warship launched, every rocket fired signifies, in the final sense, a theft from those who hunger and are not fed, those who are cold and are

Herblock's cartoon "With the Greatest of Ease" summed up the 1956 election. Ike's grip on the voters was firm, but his coattails could not carry other Republican aspirants. For the first time in over a century a re-elected President did not carry in majorities in both houses of the Congress.

© 1956, CARTOON FROM *Herblock's Special for Today,* SIMON & SCHUSTER, 1958

not clothed. . . . The cost of one modern heavy bomber is this: a modern brick school in more than thirty cities. . . . We pay for a single fighter plane with a half-million bushels of wheat. We pay for a single destroyer with new homes that could have housed more than eight thousand people." Humanity, he had said, hung from a "cross of iron." He had proposed universal disarmament.

During the presidential campaign, Eisenhower had pledged "peace and prosperity." As he left civil rights largely to the Supreme Court and to local authorities, and McCarthy to the Army, he left the engineering of prosperity to Secretary of the Treasury George Humphrey. In spite of Eisenhower's often-stated dislike for the welfare state, New Deal policies were continued. Ten million people were added to the Social Security rolls during his two terms; student loans were made available through the National Defense Education Act of 1958; and the Department of Health, Education, and Welfare was created.

The President himself concentrated on his search for peace, maneuvering around the "brinks" and over the "summits" of international diplomacy. It was the one area in which he took sufficient pains to create a novel proposal and to follow it up with his

957

Castro (above) took over Cuba early in 1959; that autumn the Khrushchevs (below) came to America.

Francis Gary Powers' trial as a U-2 spy in 1960 (below) dashed hopes for a thaw in the cold war.

own specific suggestions. "The United States pledges before you," he said in an address to the United Nations in December of 1953, " ... its determination to help solve the fearful atomic dilemma—to devote its entire heart and mind to find the way by which the miraculous inventiveness of man shall not be dedicated to his death, but consecrated to his life." He proposed a stockpile of atomic materials for peaceful purposes. That proposal, along with his attempts to effect a disarmament treaty, died a-borning. His failure to make headway in what he considered his preeminent task resulted in the most subdued passage in Eisenhower's memoirs: "In the end our accomplishments were meager, almost negligible.... the most significant, possibly the only, achievement of the entire effort was the wider education of all civilized peoples in the growing need for disarmament...." In this "bleak" defeat, Eisenhower admitted candidly, "I suffered my greatest disappointment."

Several months after the first of the Geneva Summit Conferences convened in 1955 and failed to produce any easing of cold-war tension, Eisenhower was struck with a coronary occlusion. He was hospitalized early on the morning of September 24, 1955, emerged a month later in bright red pajamas bearing the legend "Much Better, Thanks," and finally returned to the White House on November 11. His attack and temporary disability raised the question of how the business of the President was to be handled when he could not perform his duties, a question that would be resolved by a new constitutional amendment passed in 1967. It also raised the question of whether or not he would seek re-election in 1956. On February 29, 1956, he announced that "my answer will be positive, that is, affirmative." Then on June 7, he suffered an attack of ileitis that required an emergency operation. His two illnesses only enhanced the love the electorate bore him, and—after weathering a "dump Nixon" movement—the Eisenhower team was returned to office with a plurality over Adlai Stevenson, the Democratic candidate, of more than nine and a half million votes.

At the end of Eisenhower's first term the world witnessed one of the most pointless and tragic consequences of the misunderstandings of the cold war. On January 27, 1953, John Foster Dulles had announced by radio to the people of Eastern Europe that they could count on the United States for support in throwing off Soviet domination. A bill was introduced in Congress (it became known as the Captive Peoples Resolution) deploring "the forcible absorption of free peoples into an aggressive despotism." When Stalin died in March of that year, the resolution was shelved, but in April Eisenhower again called for "full independence of the East European nations." In June, however, when East Germans rioted, Eisenhower refused to intervene. Then the new Soviet leaders began to relax their hold on Eastern Europe, hoping that by easing the pressure on their captive nations they could avoid an explosion. In 1956 Khrushchev denounced Stalin and Stalinism at the Twentieth Party Congress and called, as Louis J. Halle has said, "for greater individual liberty." In April, 1956, the Cominform was dissolved, and in October Poland declared itself a neutral state. The Poles attested to their friendship with Russia—but gained some measure of dignity in their stand. In Hungary, meanwhile, all the signals from America and Russia were read incorrectly, and the Hungarians declared their own independence from Russia in November, 1956. The Red army (200,000 troops with 2,500 tanks and armored cars) moved into Budapest in the early morning of November 4 and did not leave until 32,000 people had been killed, more than 195,000 had fled their homeland, and Hungary had been returned to despotism. The two great powers, ever suspicious of each other and increasingly moralistic in their criticisms of each other, were laboring toward a *détente*. As they did so, they misled Hungary into a suicidal position—and drew back once again to their mutually hostile postures.

More than any other single event, the launching of Sputnik I on October 4, 1957, epitomized for many of the President's crit-

ics a sense of drift in his second administration. It was not until 1954 that Eisenhower had had his "first intimation that the orbiting of an earth satellite was either feasible or desirable." Eisenhower could argue with some justification that America's lag in space exploration had begun with Truman. Yet the National Aeronautics and Space Administration was not set up until July of 1958—eight months after the Russians had launched two satellites.

Criticism intensified after the launching of Sputnik. America, it seemed, was on the defensive. Its foreign policy was a reaction to Russian initiative. Its domestic programs were responses to pressures from such groups as civil rights organizations. Its program for national defense lagged behind that of the Russians, allegedly producing a "missile gap." And its sense of adventure, represented by the exploration of space, was inert. Peace and freedom, it seemed, were slowly being eroded. Prosperity was shaky at best. (An "adjustment," or recession, began in late 1957.) The launching of Sputnik was taken to illustrate the inferiority of American education. Perhaps the most serious blow of all was psychological: it was the first time most Americans could remember that the United States was second best at something. It was a rude realization.

In November of 1957, Eisenhower suffered his third illness, a slight stroke. "Gradually," he wrote in 1960, "memory of words returned; the doctors pronounced me 95 per cent recovered and said that before long I should be completely cured. In this prediction they were not wholly accurate. From that time onward I have frequently experienced difficulty in prompt utterance of the word I seek. Even today, occasionally, I reverse syllables in a long word and at times am compelled to speak slowly and cautiously if I am to enunciate correctly. This is not, I am told, particularly noticeable to anyone else but it certainly is to me." It certainly was to others, too. Yet, Eisenhower's choice of words in speech (his writing had always been perfectly clear and had showed considerably more wit than his speeches) had never been distinguished. In the 1915 yearbook for West Point he had written a parody of his own manner of speaking: "Now, fellers, it's just like this. I've been asked to say a few words this evening about this business. Now, me and Walter Camp, we think. . . ."

In 1957, after the British, French, and Israelis had attacked Egypt because of President Nasser's seizure of the Suez Canal—and had been criticized by the United Nations and the United States—Eisenhower feared that the Middle East was open to a Communist take-over. To discourage such a power move, he promulgated what came to be known as the Eisenhower Doctrine, which stated that America would aid, financially and militarily, any country in the Middle East threatened by any other country "controlled by international communism." Thus in July, 1958, President Chamoun of Lebanon requested American forces to fend off an armed rebellion that he said had been instigated by Nasser. Ike sent the Sixth Fleet and more than fourteen thousand soldiers and Marines to Lebanon, and the crisis abated. In October, American troops were withdrawn, having proved, Ike said, "in a truly practical way that the United States was capable of supporting its friends."

Ike approached another small brink in the late summer of 1958 over Quemoy and Matsu, the offshore islands that the Communist Chinese had bombarded in 1954 and chose to shell again that August. The Nationalist Chinese had been building up forces on the islands, and it is likely that the Communists wished only to test American determination in the area. They eventually lost interest and ceased shelling the islands, "except upon unusual or ceremonial occasions," as Eisenhower wrote. They permitted, in this "Gilbert and Sullivan war," the Chinese Nationalists to resupply the islands by convoy on the odd-numbered days of the month.

Eisenhower's final attempt at a Summit Conference was set for May 16, 1960. "From the autumn of 1959 to the spring of 1960," Eisenhower wrote in *Waging Peace*, "most people of the Western world felt that a slight but discernible thaw was developing in the icy tensions . . . between the West and the Soviet Union. This impression resulted partially from Mr. Khrushchev's agreement at Camp David to remove his threat to end the presence of Allied forces in West Berlin." On May 1 a high-flying U-2 reconnaissance plane was shot down over Russia. Five days later Premier Khrushchev informed the Supreme Soviet that crucial parts of the plane were in Soviet hands, that the equipment clearly indicated the U-2 was an espionage plane, and that the pilot, Francis Gary Powers, also captured, had admitted as much. Eventually Ike acknowledged the truth but did not express regrets. The Summit collapsed, and Eisenhower gradually drew back into his role of elder statesman as Vice President Nixon carried the Republican standard into battle against John F. Kennedy.

Before he retired to Gettysburg with his wife, Eisenhower took upon himself one more important duty, that of warning the nation of the "conjunction of an immense military establishment and a large arms industry," which, he said, was "new in the American experience." "We recognize the imperative need for this development," he said in his Farewell Address. "Yet we must not fail to comprehend its grave implications. Our toil, resources, and livelihood are all involved; so is the very structure of our society. In the councils of government we must guard against the acquisition of unwarranted influence, whether sought or unsought, by the military-industrial complex. The potential for the disastrous rise of misplaced power exists and will persist. We must never let the weight of this combination endanger our liberties or democratic processes. We should take nothing for granted."

If to many historians the Eisenhower years seem years of drift and indifference, it can be said as well that Eisenhower took a nation utterly fatigued from depression and two wars, frightened of nuclear holocaust, and riven with doubt about its heritage and destiny, and kept it safe and alive until it was ready to deal with life with a new-found, youthful vigor.

—CHARLES L. MEE, JR.

Dwight D. Eisenhower

A PICTURE PORTFOLIO

*One of the most familiar—and straightfor-
ward—slogans in American campaign history*

Young Dwight (foreground above) and pals often went on fishing trips; below, he is seen as a cadet in 1915. In 1932 he was an aide to General Douglas MacArthur (right). "I studied dramatics under him for five years in Washington and four in the Philippines," remarked Eisenhower.

962

A SMALL-TOWN BOY

During Dwight Eisenhower's youth, Abilene, Kansas, was the quintessence of a rural American town. Situated near the precise geographical center of the country, it was placid, law-abiding, churchgoing. "Self-sufficiency, personal initiative, and responsibility were prized," recalled Ike's brother Milton; "radicalism was unheard of." Dwight's boyhood was a normal blend of ups and downs, of pleasure and pain. He learned the value of a dollar through the hard work it took to get one. He fought with boys from the other side of town—but they all jammed into Cecil Brooks's telegraph office to get inning-by-inning reports on World Series games. In the spring of 1903, Ike and some friends took a piece of sidewalk planking and floated down Buckeye Street, which was filled with flood waters. They were well on their way to the rampaging Smoky Hill River when they were rescued, and Ike found that initial parental relief soon gave way to punishment. In school Ike hated algebra, liked spelling and arithmetic, and struggled with penmanship. His studies stood him in good stead when he applied to West Point. (Her son safely on the Academy-bound train, pacifist Ida Eisenhower cried for the first time in Milton's memory.) On Valentine's Day of 1916 Ike proposed to Mamie Doud, and on their wedding day a few months later he was promoted to first lieutenant. Ike had a stateside assignment during World War I; thereafter, despite such high points as being cited for "unusual intelligence and constant devotion to duty" by General Pershing, he often was in the doldrums as a peacetime officer. But he stuck with it, and during his tour of the Philippines with General MacArthur in the thirties he noted Japan's military build-up. Late in 1939 colleagues tagged him Alarmist Ike as he warned of inevitable American involvement in World War II. The Louisiana war-games exercises of 1941 first put Eisenhower in the public eye; he was to remain there for two decades.

UNITED PRESS INTERNATIONAL

Mamie Doud, eighteen when the photograph above was taken in 1915, was the belle of San Antonio. Once Ike had to make a date with her a month ahead.

"I HATE WAR"

I am glad it suits you," said General George C. Marshall to Eisenhower, referring to a directive on the role of the commander—whoever it would be—of the new European Theater of Operations, "because these are the orders you're going to operate under." It was mid-1942, and in London (and later at various fronts) ETO Commander Eisenhower's greatest task would be fostering a spirit of Allied unity. Over the next few years his conscientiousness, tactfulness, and ability to inspire creative compromise kept the Allied gears well oiled and well meshed. War-battered Britons liked his "breezy charm" (he had said his luxury suite at Claridge's was like "living in sin" and had moved to more modest quarters); the press called him a happy blend of an "intelligent Oxford don" and a "Rotarian speaker." But Eisenhower was also a forceful general. In late 1942 he flew to Gibraltar to oversee the start of Operation TORCH, which, by the following May, drove the Nazis out of North Africa. During the subsequent Italian campaign, Ike was given command of Supreme Headquarters of the Allied Expeditionary Forces. OVERLORD, the cross-Channel assault on Hitler's Fortress Europe, was Eisenhower's concern. He increased OVERLORD's forces to five divisions (an earlier plan—"fatally weak," he said—had called for three) and had to sweat out last-minute weather changes before beachheads were established on June 6, 1944. Early in the following year the Allies thwarted Adolph Hitler's final offensive, and in May Germany surrendered. General Eisenhower was the incarnation of the Allied triumph, but he said honestly, "I hate war as only a soldier who has lived it can, only as one who has seen its brutality, its futility, its *stupidity*."

Above, the SHAEF command plans the Normandy invasion early in 1944. Field Marshal Sir Bernard Montgomery is seated at Ike's left; he is also standing behind him in the picture below, in which the commander talks to the troops before OVERLORD.

As spring came to war-weary Europe in 1945, German cities were captured at the rate of nearly one a day. By mid-April, Seventh Army troops, right, were patrolling the streets of devastated Waldenburg.

After the war Eisenhower received Russia's Order of Victory (above left); it was the first time a foreigner had won the medal. The Commander in Chief adds an oak-leaf cluster to Ike's Distinguished Service Medal, above right. Below, in Kansas City, Missouri, a victorious Ike responds to the cheers of a nation.

"HERO AND SAVIOR"

A Roper Poll in mid-1948 showed Dwight Eisenhower to be the favorite of both parties in that year's presidential race. Ike had returned to an adoring America. He had survived a stint as chief of staff, with its vexing problems of demobilization and of the consolidation of all branches of the military under a single Department of Defense. In October, 1948, he became president of Columbia University, having stopped the draft-Ike movements with a firm statement that he would not accept nomination. When, in 1951, President Truman sent Ike to Europe to head the NATO forces, the stage was set for the repetition of what Marquis Childs referred to as "the Toynbeean withdrawal and return of the hero and savior, a rhythm of the first importance in Eisenhower's career." In January, 1952, Ike confirmed Senator Henry Cabot Lodge's summary of his "political convictions" by agreeing to accept the Republican presidential nomination if it was offered to him. A Herblock cartoon that year showed Eisenhower standing on the European shore and pondering an American coastline studded with microphones as a companion asked him, "All Ready for D-Day?"

Above, the university's president and its coach, Lou Little, watch Columbia's 1948 varsity. Early in his Army career, Ike had coached a football team.

Happy candidates Dwight Eisenhower and Richard Nixon pose with their wives on the G.O.P. convention platform on July 12, 1952. The previous day Minnesota had switched its votes from Harold Stassen to Ike, initiating a first-ballot stampede.

A FINE IMPRESSION

In 1909 a reviewer for an Abilene newspaper said that in the senior-class play Dwight Eisenhower "gave an impression that many professionals fail to reach." The critic might have repeated those words in 1952 when Eisenhower, indisputably an amateur in politics, left an impression that few pros could have bettered. The G.O.P. had been out of office for two decades, and lacked appealing candidates; Senator Robert Taft, "Mr. Republican," was unable to prevent Ike's first-ballot nomination. Commented The Washington *Post*, "It is no exaggeration to say that his nomination reflects the dominant mood of the country." Aroused by Senator Joseph McCarthy's spectacular investigations, dismayed by the mink-coat and deep-freeze scandals and the exposure of "influence peddlers" in Washington, frustrated by the Korean War and the Communist take-over in China, the nation's voters wanted a change. It was not, however, all smooth sailing for Eisenhower, an inexperienced campaigner. He was sometimes nervous before TV cameras, and he did not always field nettlesome questions deftly; the Scripps-Howard newspaper chain said, "Ike is running like a dry creek." But he learned fast and realized that he had to create party unity. He handled the corruption charge made against his running mate, Richard Nixon, with kid gloves and endorsed the re-election bids of Senator Joe McCarthy and Senator William Jenner of Indiana, another superpatriot. Some saw these stances as a lowering of the Eisenhower integrity, but most Republicans stayed with him because of his personal magnetism and the victory it promised them. In the November election, the nation embraced its hero, a man it hoped could lead as well in peace as he had in war.

At right, some of 1952's bumper crop of campaign items: Ike buttons in Spanish and Hebrew, a G.O.P. stocking, and a simulated diamond and ruby pin.

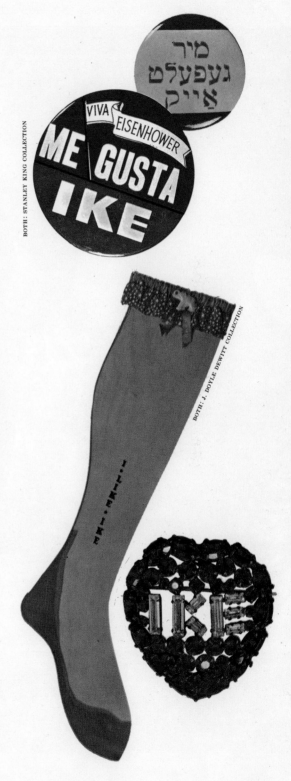

TAFT

"MR. REPUBLICAN"

I don't know what I'll do without him," lamented President Eisenhower upon the death of Senator Robert A. Taft in 1953. A year earlier the two men had been rivals for the Republican presidential nomination, and Taft had been bitterly disappointed by his defeat. Only after Eisenhower's endorsement of a number of Taft's policies did the senator offer his support. Once an agreement had been reached, however, Taft devoted his full energies to pushing the Eisenhower program through the Senate. "No twentieth-century President," wrote historian Stephen Hess, "has had a more effective legislative leader."

Taft came by his leadership abilities naturally. His grandfather, Alphonso Taft, had been President Grant's Attorney General and later minister to Austria and Russia; his father, William Howard Taft, had been President of the United States and Chief Justice of the Supreme Court. Like those distinguished statesmen, Robert Taft began his career as a lawyer. After studying at Yale and Harvard, he established a practice in Cincinnati, Ohio, and in 1921 he was elected to the state legislature. In 1938 he entered the United States Senate, where his best-known piece of legislation was the Taft-Hartley Act of 1947, designed to check the power of unions. Although Taft was a conservative Republican, his Senate career was not without its inconsistencies. As a laissez-faire economist he was vehemently opposed to the national recovery and relief programs of the New Deal; yet he supported federal aid for housing and education. An isolationist, he opposed lend-lease, selective service, and major foreign aid programs; but though he criticized the Truman Doctrine, which extended aid for the containment of communism abroad, he was tolerant of the McCarthy investigations at home. Perhaps the greatest paradox of all, however, was summed up in an observation by John F. Kennedy: "The late Senator Robert A. Taft of Ohio was never President of the United States. Therein lies his personal tragedy. And therein lies his national greatness." For although Taft was an astute politician, he had a sense of integrity and statesmanship that came before any political consideration. He stated his views in bold, blunt terms no matter how unpopular they might have been. "It is not honest to be tactful," he once said. So although he was revered in the Senate as a man of honor, logic, and impeccable honesty, "Mr. Republican," as he came to be known, was three times defeated for his party's presidential nomination—in 1940 by Wendell Willkie, in 1948 by Thomas Dewey, and in 1952 by Dwight D. Eisenhower. "It kills me to have to do this to him," groaned one Taft delegate as he switched his vote to Eisenhower. But the Republicans wanted a winner, and Ike's argument, "Taft can't win," was effective.

Taft spent the last year of his life in the service of the new President. As Senate floor leader, he was of inestimable value to Eisenhower. And in spite of some basic differences on budget and foreign policy, Eisenhower accepted the senator's conservative counsel on many important issues. Then in April, 1953, Taft felt the first pain of fatal cancer in his hip; three months later he was dead. Few senators have been mourned as Taft was. His colleagues named him the most outstanding senator of all time, and a massive Robert A. Taft monument was erected on the Capitol grounds. "The American people have lost a truly great citizen," eulogized Eisenhower, "and I have lost a wise counselor and valued friend. . . ."

Deane Keller's fresco of Taft is in the United States Capitol.

Eisenhower had promised that he would go to Korea, and in December of 1952 the President-elect did just that; the picture on the right shows him there. Negotiations to end the Korean conflict were already in progress.

The new President's Cabinet and other advisers sat for the picture below in May of 1953. Clockwise from Henry Cabot Lodge II, lower left, they are Douglas McKay, George M. Humphrey, Richard Nixon, Herbert Brownell, Sinclair Weeks, Oveta Culp Hobby, Sherman Adams, Joseph M. Dodge, Arthur S. Flemming, Martin P. Durkin, Arthur Summerfield, John Foster Dulles, President Eisenhower, Charles E. Wilson, Ezra Taft Benson, and Harold E. Stassen.

ROCKY ROADS

The new President saw himself as a symbol of national unity, but his hopes for ushering in a new Era of Good Feelings were soon dashed. He was criticized for selecting a Cabinet filled with businessmen ("eight millionaires and a plumber," said one newspaper—the plumber being Martin Durkin, ex-president of the Journeymen Plumbers and Steamfitters Union, who resigned as Secretary of Labor in less than a year). Defense Secretary Charles Wilson's controversial views, expressed with energetic candor, prompted the joke that at General Motors he had invented the automatic transmission so that he would have one foot free to put in his mouth. Joseph McCarthy, far from showing gratitude for Ike's campaign endorsement, stepped up his witch hunt, to the enduring discomfort of the President and to the detriment of morale wherever the senator struck. Democrats laughed up their sleeves when the Republican "soil bank" program looked more like a New Deal measure than a product of the administration's much-touted "dynamic conservatism." There were loud cries of "Give-away Program" as Eisenhower's conservation and power-source policies tended to favor private enterprise. So it went for Ike in civilian boot camp. But if the road to domestic tranquillity was rocky, it was not nearly so tortuous as the path to international peace.

Aide Roy Cohn (above, right) whispers to Senator Joseph McCarthy during the televised Army hearings of 1954. President Eisenhower refused to censure McCarthy openly because, as he told friends, he did not care to "get in the gutter" with him.

LAUREATES

CARL SANDBURG

Carl Sandburg, who was born in Illinois in 1878, became the celebrant of America's heartland—of its common man, its awesome machinery, its vast plains. In idiomatic, muscular free verse, he described Chicago: "Hog Butcher for the World . . . Stormy, husky, brawling, City of the Big Shoulders . . . Flinging magnetic curses amid the toil of piling job on job, here is a tall bold slugger set vivid against the little soft cities. . . ." To Sandburg the prairie was "an ocean of to-morrows, a sky of to-morrows." After leaving Lombard College without a degree, Sandburg pursued a journalism career; his poems were widely published after 1914 and he became a member of the "Chicago group" of writers. The mood of his poems ranges from whimsey, in "Fog," to excoriation, in "To a Contemporary Bunkshooter," which concerns Billy Sunday. Sandburg spent thirty years researching and writing a six-volume biography of Abraham Lincoln that won a Pulitzer Prize in 1940. He was awarded another Pulitzer following the publication of *Complete Poems* in 1950. Sandburg also gathered folk ballads for his *American Song-bag* and wrote the charming *Rootabaga Stories* for children. He spent his later years in North Carolina and in 1953 published the autobiographical *Always the Young Strangers*.

WILLIAM FAULKNER

"I believe that man will not merely endure: he will prevail . . . because he has a soul, a spirit capable of compassion and sacrifice . . ." said William Faulkner in 1950 as he accepted a Nobel Prize for literature. Faulkner's words, and the award itself, surprised a large percentage of the American public, who regarded his works about mythical Yoknapatawpha County in his native Mississippi as epics of human degradation. His first commercially successful book, *Sanctuary* (1931), was a macabre rendering of the same grim environment that he had already described in *Sartoris*, *The Sound and the Fury*, and *As I Lay Dying*. But underlying the endless struggles of his characters—fallen Southern aristocrats, newly rich white trash, and Negroes who either "knew their place" or did not—is an extraordinary ability to survive; with each generation new orders replace old. In his intricate, innovational, and often abstruse style, Faulkner subsequently followed the fortunes—and the passions and aberrations—of several families in a number of interlocking novels, principally *Absalom, Absalom!*, *The Unvanquished*, and a trilogy comprising *The Hamlet*, *The Town*, and *The Mansion*. William Faulkner died in 1962; he was awarded a posthumous Pulitzer Prize for *The Reivers*.

ERNEST HEMINGWAY

ROBERT FROST

Although Ernest Hemingway was in the vanguard of the Paris-based American expatriate writers after World War I, he was more an American than a man of the world. His heroes—almost all Americans—are hard but not cynical, idealistic but practical, and, somehow, innocent. His first principal hero, Nick Adams of *In Our Time*, hunts, fishes, and sees animals being born and dying, as Hemingway had done during his childhood. In *The Sun Also Rises* and *A Farewell to Arms* the author's protagonists are victimized but self-sufficient Americans, generally making do in the world that has victimized them. Writing in lean, colloquial, and unique prose, Hemingway gradually involved his heroes in their own destinies: Robert Jordan, of *For Whom the Bell Tolls*, fights, and then dies, for a belief. After 1940 Hemingway's career seemed to be dying, too; although he kept busy doing the masculine things his heroes did—hunting, fishing, drinking—he did very little good writing. In 1952, however, he published *The Old Man and the Sea*, in which his first major non-American hero, a Cuban fisherman, wages an eventually disastrous, but always noble and dignified, battle against the sea. The book was awarded the Nobel Prize for literature in 1954. Painfully ill, Hemingway killed himself in 1961.

"To me," Robert Frost once said, "the thing that art does for life is to clean it, to strip it to form." His own economical, stripped-down poetry was for him "a reaching out toward expression. . . ." He said that "a complete poem is one where an emotion has found its thought and the thought has found the words." Frost's personal reaching-out process was long. Born in California and raised in New England, he attended Dartmouth and Harvard and worked at several jobs before traveling to England in 1912. Two volumes of poetry, *A Boy's Will* and *North of Boston*, made him famous by the time he returned home in 1915. Dealing with universal themes in the clipped, colloquial language of New England, his poetry was clear, understated, well metered, its symbols generally restricted to the commonplace occurrences of rural America. At a metaphorical fork in a woodland road, he chose "the one less traveled by/And that has made all the difference." Although his later work was somewhat more obscure, most of his poems are, as critic C. Henry Warren put it, "as direct and unmoral as the song of a bird." Four times a Pulitzer Prize winner, Frost recited his "The Gift Outright" at President John F. Kennedy's inauguration. He died at the age of eighty-eight in 1963.

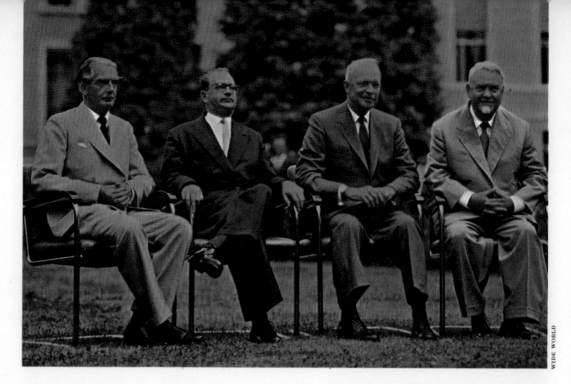

At the Summit in 1955 were, above from the left, Anthony
Eden of England, Edgar Fauré of France, President
Dwight D. Eisenhower, and Nikolai Bulganin of Russia.
The good will of Geneva was short-lived: in 1956 Brit-
ain and France were bearing arms, right, in Suez.

After the division of Indochina in 1954, the People's
Army had no trouble (above) taking over North Vietnam.

THEORY AND PRACTICE

Almost from the start, demands were heard for the ouster of John Foster Dulles, Eisenhower's trusted shaper of foreign policy. "Hard" on communism, Dulles was unwilling to negotiate with the Red bloc, which, in his moralistic view, was an evil that surely would crumble under America's potential for "massive retaliation." (Russia's development of the same potential did not alter the Dulles line.) He spoke of recapturing the "crusading spirit of the early days of the Republic," but in only a few cases did the administration boldly implement its stated policy of brinkmanship. The gap between theory and practice shook the free world's faith in American leadership. Uneasy peaces left Korea and Indochina breeding grounds for further flare-ups of hot warfare; in 1956 Hungary found it could not count on the United States when the fat was in the fire; that year, too, the United States call for a cease-fire in Suez—however just—antagonized Britain and France, her two firmest allies. But if Dulles was having his problems, the view from the Summit was hardly any clearer. At Geneva in 1955 Eisenhower concluded, "It is not always necessary that people should think alike and believe alike before they can work together"; this flimsy "spirit of Geneva" would afford little protection against the continuing chill of the long cold war.

Russian tanks roll through Budapest, above, putting down the Hungarian uprising of 1956. The United Nations issued a protest, and President Eisenhower said, "The heart of America goes out to the people of Hungary."

"THE VIRUS OF MORALITY"

A funny thing happened to me on the way to the White House!" said Adlai Stevenson after the presidential election of 1952. "I was happy to hear that I had even placed second."

Stevenson had not wanted the Democratic nomination in the first place. He had hoped to be re-elected governor of Illinois; he had been uncertain of his ability to serve as President; he had been reluctant to oppose the probable Republican candidate, General Dwight Eisenhower, the popular war hero who was, according to Stevenson, as familiar as "the catchup bottle on the kitchen table." Despite his reluctance, Stevenson had been drafted by the Democrats and, as expected, had been badly beaten.

But curiously, when President Eisenhower, more popular than ever, stood for re-election four years later, Adlai Ewing Stevenson actively sought his party's nomination, won it, and leaped into a campaign that offered him virtually no chance of victory. Against the wishes of his advisers, the former Chicago lawyer and diplomat aimed his attacks not only at the administration in general but at the popular Ike in particular; and he raised the important but avoidable issue of nuclear fallout. Eisenhower called Stevenson's request for an end to atmospheric testing of nuclear bombs a "moratorium on common sense." (Two years later, Ike would make the same proposal.) Typical of the odds against which Stevenson was running was a series of crises in the Middle East—just two weeks before Election Day—which, although largely the result of administration blunders, served to further solidify the American people behind President Eisenhower. Stevenson carried only seven states in the November election.

Theodore H. White once suggested that Stevenson placed "the virus of morality in the bloodstream of both parties." While the urbane Stevenson, namesake of a grandfather who had been Grover Cleveland's second Vice President, was himself too genuinely humble to admit that that was his aim, it was probably the reason why he sought a hopeless candidacy. Condemning the use of "soft soap, slogans, gimmicks, bandwagons and all the other infernal machines of modern high-pressure politics" as "contempt for people's intelligence, common sense and dignity," he introduced a wit, an eloquence, and a moral tone to campaigning that had not before been present. And because he respected the people whose support he sought, he became not the postelection recluse and public joke that two-time losers so often become, but, as Walter Lippmann put it, "a living specimen of the kind of American that Americans themselves, and the great mass of mankind, would like to think that Americans are."

In 1961 Stevenson wanted to be Secretary of State, but President John Kennedy appointed him ambassador to the United Nations. During the Cuban Missile Crisis the next year, when Soviet Ambassador Valerian Zorin hedged on Stevenson's query regarding the presence of Russian missiles in Cuba, the American ambassador cried, "I am prepared to wait for my answer until hell freezes over!" But as his role in policy making declined even more under President Johnson, the United Nations job increasingly frustrated and exhausted Stevenson. In 1965 in London, a few days before his fatal heart attack, he privately announced his intention to resign soon. "Ah, well," Stevenson sighed, "for a while, I'd really just like to sit in the shade with a glass of wine in my hand and watch the people dance."

Adlai E. Stevenson in 1952

REACTING

As his second term progressed, President Eisenhower resembled more and more the Dutch boy with his finger in the dike. While the country's problems continued to develop, the administration—marked by conservatism and an urge to decentralize—created few new federal responsibilities. Toward the end of the term, for example, the President vetoed a bill aimed at making the federal government responsible for coping with the pollution of rivers. In his veto message Eisenhower declared: "Because water pollution is a uniquely local blight, primary responsibility . . . must be assumed . . . by State and local governments . . . and industry." The trouble was that many local officials and businessmen refused to accept the burden, and water pollutants continued to pour into the nation's rivers. Clearly, if the situation were left as it was, it would eventually deteriorate until the federal government would *have* to take charge. Thus instead of appearing dynamic by thrusting duty on the states and cities, the administration was criticized for trapping itself into acting defensively. Similarly, Eisenhower did little, through moral persuasion or otherwise, to bring about desegregation of schools in the South until—three years after the Supreme Court decision ordering integration—Governor Orval Faubus of Arkansas called out the National Guard to defy a federal court order, thereby compelling Eisenhower to send federal troops to Little Rock and to federalize the National Guard there. And it took the launching of the Russian Sputniks to spur the Eisenhower administration into two of its most important accomplishments: the creation of the National Aeronautics and Space Administration and the strengthening of American education, particularly in the sciences.

At left, an American satellite is launched in 1958. Right, the Arkansas National Guard, federalized by President Eisenhower, keeps the peace at Central High School in Little Rock in September, 1957.

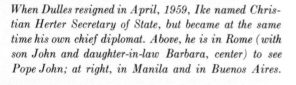

When Dulles resigned in April, 1959, Ike named Christian Herter Secretary of State, but became at the same time his own chief diplomat. Above, he is in Rome (with son John and daughter-in-law Barbara, center) to see Pope John; at right, in Manila and in Buenos Aires.

A HARRIED LEADER

Eisenhower, despite his uncertain health, had to lead in a world that expected a great deal from the United States. International confidence was shaken in November, 1957, by the President's third serious illness—a mild stroke; it occurred less than three weeks before a scheduled meeting of the NATO heads of state. (Told by doctors that he could not go to a state dinner the night of the stroke, he fumed, "If I cannot attend to my duties, I am simply going to give up this job.") He recovered rapidly and he helped make the NATO conference a success. But the "missile gap" and Russia's lead in the space race were constantly troubling. And not long after the stroke, Richard Nixon's trip to South America revealed strong anti-American sentiment there. Late in the summer of 1958 the mainland Chinese began heavy shelling of the islands of Quemoy and Matsu; the Seventh Fleet was posted to shepherd anti-invasion troops from Taiwan to the offshore islands. There was no invasion, but there was considerable criticism abroad of American actions. Khrushchev's threat to turn over to East Germany the access routes to Berlin was withdrawn at Camp David in September, 1959, but the thaw ended when an American spy plane was shot down over Russia in 1960. A poll that year showed American prestige overseas in marked decline. Perhaps Eisenhower could have prevented some of the prestige loss. Still, his difficulties demonstrated what Pakistan's President Ayub Khan referred to as America's unique role. Because it was powerful *and* democratic, the United States was "placed in the unenviable position of returning hostility with consideration, coldness with warmth, indifference with attention, and friendship, of course, with friendship."

In India in 1959, Ike (being introduced at the University of New Delhi, left) was met by what Jawaharlal Nehru (seated) called India's greatest demonstration since its independence day in 1950.

983

WASHINGTON FACES

OMAR N. BRADLEY

Musing over the contention that successful battle strategy is best conceived at a distance from the heart-wrenching realities of death and injury in the field, Omar Nelson Bradley once remarked that war is fought by men and is "as much a conflict of passion as it is of force. . . . Far from being a handicap to command, compassion is the measure of it." Combat reporter Ernie Pyle met the tenor-voiced Missourian during World War II and wrote: "I don't believe I have ever known a person so unanimously loved and respected by the men around and under him." Born in 1893, Bradley was a member of the same West Point class as Dwight Eisenhower. He rose slowly in the peacetime Army until, in February, 1941, he was made commandant of the Infantry School at Fort Benning, Georgia, and became the first member of the class of 1915 to be promoted to star rank. World War II saw Bradley rise from command of a division to command of the Twelfth Army Group—four armies that drove northward across Europe into Germany. A four-star general by V-E Day (he was awarded a fifth in 1950), he served successively as administrator of veterans' affairs, as Army chief of staff, and, from 1949 to 1953, as the first chairman of the joint chiefs of staff. Bradley retired in 1953 and subsequently became a business executive.

J. EDGAR HOOVER

"The Federal Bureau of Investigation, the G-men and Mr. J. Edgar Hoover," said British writer Cyril Connolly, "form one of the most important elements of the American myth—symbols of perfection in detective methods, wholesome anticommunism, ruthless pursuit of gangsters and spies, and of a dedicated, puritanical but unselfseeking chief above and outside politics. . . ." John Edgar Hoover's home, from the day of his birth, January 1, 1895, was Washington, D.C. He attended public school there and worked his way through George Washington University, receiving his master of laws degree in 1917. A special assistant to Attorney General A. Mitchell Palmer during the Red Scare of the Wilson administration, he was made head of the FBI in 1924, at the age of twenty-nine. The bureau came to bear his stamp in everything: its special training courses and advanced methods of detective work, its thoroughness, the high level of honesty on the part of its agents, and its conservatism in politics. Through its successes against crime and its carefully handled public relations Hoover grew to have considerable influence in Congress and a large measure of autonomy in the government. He had a marked ability to survive in office despite criticism of his attitudes and power by civil libertarians.

JOHN FOSTER DULLES

"Foster has been studying to be Secretary of State since he was five years old," President Eisenhower once said of John Foster Dulles. Actually, Dulles began his diplomatic career at the age of nineteen when he attended the Hague Conference in 1907 as secretary to the Chinese delegation. He served in World War I and was one of Wilson's advisers on the Versailles Treaty. Thereafter he became a leading international lawyer. He served as a delegate to the United Nations from 1946 to 1950, and in 1951 he negotiated the Japanese Peace Treaty. Appointed Secretary of State in 1953, Dulles was given unprecedented authority in shaping American foreign policy during the Eisenhower administration. "I think he is the wisest, most dedicated man that I know," avowed the President. Although few took issue with his dedication, many critics questioned the wisdom of Dulles' doctrine of massive retaliation as a deterrent to Communist aggression—particularly in view of the Soviet Union's nuclear power and Dulles' willingness to go to the "brink of war" if necessary. During his six-year tenure, Dulles was instrumental in holding back Chinese Communist aggression at Quemoy and Matsu and in halting the Anglo-French seizure of the Suez Canal. Dulles died in May, 1959, after treatment for a malignant tumor.

EARL WARREN

The appointment of Governor Earl Warren as Chief Justice of the Supreme Court put the capstone on a career devoted to politics and public service. Warren, the son of Scandinavian immigrants, was born in 1891 in Los Angeles. Educated in public schools and at the University of California, he was awarded his law degree in 1914. In 1925 he became district attorney of Alameda County, serving in that position until he won election as California attorney general in 1938. He was elected governor in 1942, 1946, and 1950. Warren was the state's favorite son at the Republican National Conventions of 1944 and 1948 and was Thomas Dewey's running mate in the 1948 campaign. After Chief Justice Fred Vinson died, President Eisenhower, in September, 1953, appointed Warren to replace him. The next May Warren read the Court's unanimous decision nullifying the legitimacy of "separate but equal" (segregated) public education. This and other liberal decisions by the Court brought demands by ultraconservatives for Warren's impeachment. But perhaps the most trying assignment of Warren's life was the chairmanship of the commission investigating President Kennedy's assassination; the commission failed to lay to rest national doubts about the sad event, and was the subject of a heated controversy.

985

Golfer Eisenhower is shown above in 1964—playing in a benefit match for the Heart Fund. Painter Eisenhower made the portrait of Lincoln below from an 1863 photograph.

"YOU DO NOT LEAD BY HITTING PEOPLE"

Dwight Eisenhower was indebted to the military, for it had given him a career that had led to the Presidency; he was also, to a great extent, sympathetic to private enterprise. Yet as he left the White House in 1961, he warned the nation of the dangers inherent in a society dominated by a "military-industrial complex." He was not turning against those who had made him a public figure or sustained him in public office; he was reasserting his primary allegiance—to the best interests, as he saw them, of the nation as a whole. This enduring attitude helps to explain Eisenhower's attempts to remain above partisan politics, to embody a unified America rather than a single political party. He had a textbook concept of the division of power in federal government and seldom tried to force measures through the national legislature. ("You do not lead by hitting people over the head," he often said, although once he admitted that dealing with a Democratic Congress was "no bed of roses.") Nevertheless, his two administrations were not without accomplishments. Social Security was expanded; the minimum wage was raised to a dollar an hour; two civil rights bills were passed; an Air Force Academy and the Department of Health, Education, and Welfare were created; the St. Lawrence seaway project was authorized and completed. Eisenhower's foreign policy record and his failure to act at home when action seemed to many to be desperately needed have often been criticized. But postwar America had wanted a President in whom the average citizen could place absolute confidence. Eisenhower had filled the bill and had done his best to continue the nation's progress toward "the great destiny for which she was created."

Presidents Kennedy and Johnson periodically sought Eisenhower's views; the former Chief Executive walks with John Kennedy, right, at Camp David during the Cuban Missile Crisis of 1962.

FACTS IN SUMMARY: DWIGHT D. EISENHOWER

CHRONOLOGY

UNITED STATES		EISENHOWER				
Sherman Antitrust Act	1890	*Born October 14*	Truman elected	1948	*Named president of Columbia University*	
	1911	*Enters U.S. Military Academy*	Korean War begins	1950		
				1951	*Commands SHAPE*	
Lusitania sunk	1915	*Commissioned 2nd lt.*		1952	*Elected President*	
Wilson re-elected	1916	*Marries Mamie Doud*			*Visits Korea*	
Second Battle of the Marne	1918	*Commands tank-training center*	Armistice signed in Korea	1953	*Names Earl Warren Chief Justice*	
	1922	*Assigned to Panama*	Supreme Court orders school desegregation	1954	*Refuses to condemn Senator McCarthy*	
	1925	*Attends Command and General Staff School*	Army-McCarthy hearings		*Gives air support to French in Indochina*	
Hoover elected President	1928	*Writes guide to French battlefields*	SEATO pact signed			
Stock market crash	1929	*Works in office of asst. secretary of war*		1955	*Attends Summit Conference at Geneva*	
Franklin Roosevelt elected President	1932	*Attached to staff of Gen. Douglas MacArthur*			*Suffers heart attack*	
Social Security Act	1935	*Assigned to Philippines*	Hungarian Revolt	1956	*Re-elected President*	
World War II begins	1939	*Returns to U.S.*	Suez Crisis		*Undergoes operation for ileitis*	
Roosevelt re-elected	1940	*Named chief of staff of Third Division*	Civil Rights Commission established	1957	*Announces Eisenhower Doctrine*	
War with Japan and Germany	1941	*Wins mock battle in Louisiana*	Soviets launch Sputnik I		*Sends troops to Little Rock, Ark.*	
Battle of Bataan	1942	*Named assistant chief of staff to Gen. Marshall*	Business recession		*Proposes nuclear test ban*	
Operation TORCH					*Suffers stroke*	
Battle of Guadalcanal		*Assumes command of ETO*	Explorer I launched	1958	*Sends U.S. troops to Lebanon*	
		Directs invasion of North Africa	NASA created			
			Red Chinese shell Quemoy and Matsu			
Battle of Tarawa	1943	*Directs invasions of Sicily and Italy*	Alaska and Hawaii admitted to Union	1959	*Meets Khrushchev at Camp David*	
Italian Campaign						
D-Day	1944	*Named supreme commander of A.E.F.*	U-2 incident	1960	*Visits South America*	
Battle of Leyte Gulf			Kennedy elected President			
Battle of the Bulge		*Directs Normandy invasion*	Bay of Pigs	1961	*Retires to Gettysburg*	
Truman becomes President	1945	*Accepts surrender of Germany*	Johnson becomes President	1963		
A-bombs dropped on Japan		*Becomes chief of staff, U.S. Army*	Vietnam War intensified	1966	*Undergoes gall bladder operation*	

CARLA DAVIDSON COLLECTION

Alaska and Hawaii, the forty-ninth and fiftieth states, were admitted to the Union in Eisenhower's second term.

BIOGRAPHICAL FACTS

BIRTH: Denison, Texas, Oct. 14, 1890

ANCESTRY: Swiss-German

FATHER: David Jacob Eisenhower; b. Elizabethville, Pa., Sept. 23, 1863; d. Abilene, Kan., March 10, 1942

FATHER'S OCCUPATION: Mechanic

MOTHER: Ida Elizabeth Stover Eisenhower; b. Mount Sidney, Va., May 1, 1862; d. Abilene, Kan., Sept. 11, 1946

BROTHERS: Arthur (1886–1958); Edgar (1889–   ); Roy (1892–1942); Earl (1898–   ); Milton (1899–   )

WIFE: Mamie Geneva Doud: b. Boone, Iowa, Nov. 14, 1896

MARRIAGE: Denver, Colo., July 1, 1916

CHILDREN: Doud Dwight (1917–1921); John Sheldon (1922–   )

EDUCATION: Public schools; U.S. Military Academy, West Point, N.Y. (graduated 1915)

RELIGIOUS AFFILIATION: Presbyterian

MILITARY SERVICE: Commissioned 2nd lt. in U.S. Army (1915); served in various posts in United States, Panama, and Philippines (1915–1942); named commander of European Theater of Operations (1942); named supreme commander of Allied Expeditionary Force in Western Europe (1943); promoted to general of the Army (1944); named Army chief of staff (1945); appointed supreme commander of Allied powers in Europe (1951)

AGE AT INAUGURATION: 62

OCCUPATION AFTER PRESIDENCY: Writer

ELECTION OF 1952

CANDIDATES	ELECTORAL VOTE	POPULAR VOTE
Dwight D. Eisenhower Republican	442	33,936,234
Adlai E. Stevenson Democratic	89	27,314,992
Vincent Hallinan Progressive	—	140,023

FIRST ADMINISTRATION

INAUGURATION: January 20, 1953; the Capitol, Washington, D.C.

VICE PRESIDENT: Richard M. Nixon

SECRETARY OF STATE: John Foster Dulles

SECRETARY OF THE TREASURY: George M. Humphrey

SECRETARY OF DEFENSE: Charles E. Wilson

ATTORNEY GENERAL: Herbert Brownell, Jr.

POSTMASTER GENERAL: Arthur E. Summerfield

SECRETARY OF THE INTERIOR: Douglas McKay; Frederick A. Seaton (from June 8, 1956)

SECRETARY OF AGRICULTURE: Ezra Taft Benson

SECRETARY OF COMMERCE: Sinclair Weeks

SECRETARY OF LABOR: Martin Durkin; James P. Mitchell (from Jan. 19, 1954)

SECRETARY OF HEALTH, EDUCATION, AND WELFARE (Department created April 1, 1953): Oveta Culp Hobby; Marion B. Folsom (from Aug. 1, 1955)

SUPREME COURT APPOINTMENTS: Earl Warren, Chief Justice (1953); John M. Harlan (1955); William J. Brennan, Jr. (1956)

83rd CONGRESS (January 3, 1953–January 3, 1955):
Senate: 48 Republicans; 47 Democrats; 1 Other
House: 221 Republicans; 211 Democrats; 1 Other

84th CONGRESS (January 3, 1955–January 3, 1957):
Senate: 48 Democrats; 47 Republicans; 1 Other
House: 232 Democrats; 203 Republicans

ELECTION OF 1956

CANDIDATES	ELECTORAL VOTE	POPULAR VOTE
Dwight D. Eisenhower Republican	457	35,590,472
Adlai E. Stevenson Democratic	73	26,022,752
T. Coleman Andrews States' Rights	—	107,929

SECOND ADMINISTRATION

INAUGURATION: January 20, 1957; the Capitol, Washington, D.C.

VICE PRESIDENT: Richard M. Nixon

SECRETARY OF STATE: John Foster Dulles; Christian A. Herter (from April 22, 1959)

SECRETARY OF THE TREASURY: George M. Humphrey; Robert B. Anderson (from July 29, 1957)

SECRETARY OF DEFENSE: Charles E. Wilson; Neil H. McElroy (from Oct. 9, 1957); Thomas S. Gates, Jr. (from Jan. 26, 1960)

ATTORNEY GENERAL: Herbert Brownell, Jr.; William P. Rogers (from Jan. 27, 1958)

POSTMASTER GENERAL: Arthur E. Summerfield

SECRETARY OF THE INTERIOR: Frederick A. Seaton

SECRETARY OF AGRICULTURE: Ezra Taft Benson

SECRETARY OF COMMERCE: Sinclair Weeks; Frederick H. Mueller (from Aug. 6, 1959)

SECRETARY OF LABOR: James P. Mitchell

SECRETARY OF HEALTH, EDUCATION, AND WELFARE: Marion B. Folsom; Arthur S. Flemming (from Aug. 1, 1958)

SUPREME COURT APPOINTMENTS: Charles E. Whittaker (1957); Potter Stewart (1958)

85th CONGRESS (January 3, 1957–January 3, 1959):
Senate: 49 Democrats; 47 Republicans
House: 233 Democrats; 200 Republicans

86th CONGRESS (January 3, 1959–January 3, 1961):
Senate: 64 Democrats; 34 Republicans
House: 283 Democrats; 153 Republicans

STATES ADMITTED: Alaska (1959); Hawaii (1959)